M000203959

SECRET COLUMBUS

A GUIDE TO THE WEIRD, WONDERFUL, AND OBSCURE

Anietra Hamper

Copyright © 2018, Reedy Press, LLC
All rights reserved.
Reedy Press
PO Box 5131
St. Louis, MO 63139
www.reedypress.com

No part of this publication may be reproduced or transmitted in any form or by any means, electronic or mechanical, including photocopy, recording, or any information storage and retrieval system, without permission in writing from the publisher. Permissions may be sought directly from Reedy Press at the above mailing address or via our website at www.reedypress.com.

Library of Congress Control Number: 2017957325

ISBN: 9781681061252

Design by Jill Halpin

Printed in the United States of America
18 19 20 21 22   5 4 3 2 1

DEDICATION

To my mom and dad, who inspired my curious mind and taught me that the world holds wondrous secrets if we only choose to look for them.

CONTENTS

INTRODUCTION

Columbus is an evolving city with a vibe that resonates from the peculiar fringe details that hover behind the obvious. The people, buildings, attractions, and notable historical moments that make up the city's diverse personality developed from unique and sometimes bizarre foundations. This obscure minutia is what splashes color onto the Columbus canvas.

Who knew that settler-era squirrel hunts, belly dancing, and trash-eating pigs would be among the underlying reasons for the evolving status quo in Columbus? *Secret Columbus* is a journey offering new perspectives on the capital city.

While the knowledge of an abandoned stretch of highway suspended above downtown, a forgotten pet cemetery with headstones detailing Fido's most notable traits, and a lost verse to Carmen Ohio may not change your life, it could alter your view of Columbus. These finds serve up the kind of personal gratification that straddles the line between enlightening and useless, but nonetheless exciting.

As a Columbus native and career investigative journalist, I leave no stone, contact, or dusty government document unturned in my pursuit of the untold and forgotten stories behind the things and places you thought you knew about Columbus.

This book is a roadmap of discovery that takes you to the corners of the metro area and suburbs with a promise of awe-inspiring enlightenment. Whether you read *Secret Columbus* cover to cover or open a page and tackle a Saturday excursion to someplace new, you will never eat a candy buckeye, walk through the Arena District, or sing the National Anthem before a baseball game the same way ever again.

¹FINDERS KEEPERS

Why are buses the focus of a secret scavenger hunt in Columbus?

Exploring the nuances of Columbus neighborhoods is the ideal way to experience the charm that each one offers. Keen observers are likely to find a little something extra if they look hard enough. Occasionally, a small wooden block sporting a picture of a school bus will pop up in the crevice of a building or on the fence bordering a bridge walkway. The small art blocks are delightful treasures from an ongoing civic project designed to make people pay closer attention to their communities.

"The Bus Project" was launched in 2007 as the brainchild of local artist Matthew Logsdon. The artifacts are small rectangles of wood about the size of a deck of cards painted with a silkscreen print of a school bus. Inspired by a passion for street art and pedestrian exploration, Logsdon created and distributed two thousand of the small buses throughout the city.

Logsdon found hiding spots in the anomalies of structures, like a missing brick, an oddly shaped pipe, a ledge, or hole in a wall. He was fond of leaving the treasures near locally owned businesses and distributed more than

Left: One of two thousand small bus paintings hidden around Columbus in pedestrian and bike-friendly locations. Credit: Matthew Logston. Right: A painted "Bus Project" block hanging on the side of a building. Credit: Matthew Logston.

A bus hidden among the bricks on the exterior of a Columbus building. Credit: Matthew Logston.

fifteen hundred of them by foot and bike. Another five hundred were distributed at the project's completion to people who signed an agreement promising to continue distributing them throughout the city.

"I left buses in pedestrian-friendly areas to draw attention to the experiences provided by walking," said Logsdon.

The thrill of finding the small bus paintings in this secret Columbus scavenger hunt combines the element of surprise and the excitement of new discoveries in neighborhoods around the city. By looking for them, pedestrians are likely to also discover the unique architecture, nature, businesses, and flavor of local communities.

Though the project officially concluded in 2011, and Logsdon has since moved to New York, the small buses are still circulating as finders of the treasures continue to redistribute them.

THE BUS PROJECT

WHAT A completed art installation project that continues to inspire neighborhood exploration

WHERE They could be anywhere in the city.

COST None

PRO TIP Start your search in Clintonville, where artist Matthew Logsdon was fond of hiding them.

The print of the school bus is symbolic of C-Bus, the nickname of Columbus.

2 UNION STATION ARCHES

How did an OSU game impact salvage efforts of the old Union Train Station arches?

The Union Station depot in Columbus was the welcome center for railroad passengers in the late 1800s. The arches that surrounded the grand rail entrance on High Street were the geographical entrance to what is now known as the Short North. One of the arches still stands in Columbus, though its purpose and location are different. The remaining arch towers over McFerson Commons Park as the classical centerpiece of the urban and edgy Arena District. An eleventh-hour legal battle that played out during an OSU football game can be credited for saving at least one of the arches from demolition and for making it a marquee landmark in the thriving Arena District.

The elaborate icon of the Arena District is the only one of the two arches that survived the Union Station demolition in 1976. The Ohio Historical Society (now the Ohio History Connection) launched an effort to save the arches from the wrecking ball but demolition day was scheduled on a game-day Saturday at OSU (OSU vs. Purdue). In Columbus, OSU game days mean that no one in the city focuses on anything else, including judges. For those fighting to save the arches, that meant that finding an available judge to sign the legal documents to halt demolition proved almost impossible.

UNION STATION ARCHES

WHAT The historic Union Station arches that are now the centerpiece of McFerson Commons Park

WHERE 218 West St. in the Arena District

COST None

PRO TIP Visit the arches at night when artistic lighting casts a nostalgic illumination on the grand pillars.

4

Union Station arches now standing at McFerson Commons Park in the Arena District.

As time ticked away, the first set of arches crumbled to the ground while the wrecking ball took aim at the second set. With literally minutes to spare, it was saved. Preservationists tracked down Judge George Tyack to sign a temporary order to halt demolition on October 23, 1976.

The stunning 1893 Union Station arches are well suited to their new home in the Arena District several blocks away from their original space. The prominent spot at McFerson Commons Park is a popular community gathering place and a welcome sight for visitors to Columbus.

The classic Neo-Roman style Union Station depot was designed by renowned architect Daniel Burnham, who is also famous for designing the World's Fair Columbian Exposition in 1893.

CIRCUS HOUSE SECRETS

An old trunk that belonged to the Sells Brothers and an original Buffalo Bill circus poster that remain in the home.

What Sells Circus secrets hide in the most recognized home in Victorian Village?

Most people refer to the whimsical brick mansion on Dennison Avenue only as the "Circus House." The history and mystery surrounding the home are as intriguing as the visual details of the Romanesque-style Frank Packard architecture.

Legendary tales of scandal and adultery add intrigue to the home built by Sells Circus owner Peter Sells for his wife, Mary, in 1895.

Some stories, like the alleged basement enclosures that housed baby elephants and other circus animals, seem too extravagant to be true. Current owner Weston Wolfe is only one of seven private owners in the home's 122-year history. That means few people have ventured inside to truly investigate.

Like a ringmaster exciting the crowd, the stories leaked to outsiders over the years have generated a curiosity about this Victorian home, leaving most to wonder which, if any, of the stories are true.

Wolfe uncovered a number of artifacts that have stayed with the home since it was built, including circus posters, handwritten letters from the Sells brothers, an original flyer for Buffalo Bill Cody, one of the biggest acts of the circus, and Peter Sells's travel chest.

And what about those animal enclosures in the basement?

Although there is no official documentation, the visual evidence suggests that it is true. I got a rare look into the

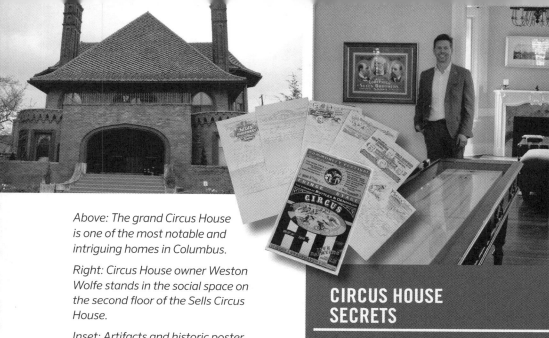

Above: The grand Circus House is one of the most notable and intriguing homes in Columbus.

Right: Circus House owner Weston Wolfe stands in the social space on the second floor of the Sells Circus House.

Inset: Artifacts and historic poster found in the Circus House.

three-layered brick basement dwellings. Notable are the two entrances and exits, extra-wide basement hallways, and a double-wide door to the outside large enough for a baby elephant. The room partitions that line the hallway are designed similar to animal enclosures.

Over the years, the home has been repurposed as a daycare, a private club for the United Commercial Travelers, a Fraternal Order of Police lodge, a food company, and a shelter for alcoholics.

CIRCUS HOUSE SECRETS

WHAT One of the most admired, recognizable and mysterious homes in the city

WHERE 755 Dennison Ave. in Victorian Village

COST The private home is not open for tours, but you can admire it for free from the sidewalk.

PRO TIP This is a private residence so admire it from the sidewalk or Goodale Park. Carriage House rooms are listed for rent on Air B&B.

The Circus House is 7,600 square feet, with an adjacent 1,650-square-foot carriage house.

4 THE SHORT NORTH NAME

How did this artsy district really get its name?

The Short North Arts District is one of the most vibrant and popular neighborhoods in Columbus, but the catchy name that fits its present-day profile is not its true identity. The name evolved out of the district's seedy past when, instead of being known for artistic eateries and galleries, the area was characterized by urban blight and overrun with crime and prostitution.

THE SHORT NORTH

WHAT An urban blight turned cosmopolitan district in Columbus

WHERE A sixteen-block stretch of N High St. starting at the Short North Cap

COST Free with the exception of shopping at one of the 320 businesses and restaurants in the area

PRO TIP The best time to experience the Short North is during the Short North Gallery Hop that takes place the first Saturday of every month. It is as exciting for the people-watching as for street entertainment and for patronizing the galleries and shops that stay open late on Hop nights.

The neighborhood, which occupies a stretch of High Street just north of the convention center, had no name in the 1960s, just a bad reputation. It was an area frequented by Columbus Police officers who repeatedly responded to calls about crimes involving drugs and prostitution.

As a result, officers needed a quick way to identify the location that was "north" of downtown and "short" of the OSU campus. Secret Columbus tracked down the longest-serving officer with the Columbus Division of Police who responded to the early "short north" dispatches.

Lieutenant Karl Barth remembers when "short north" became the quick call for

Top: The Short North's 17 lighted steel arches over High Street are the district's most notable features. Credit: Short North Alliance.

Inset: One of the streetscape murals on the sides of Short North buildings. Credit: Short North Alliance.

Columbus Police working the area. It was a time when the Short North was a hub of criminal activity, with the burlesque Garden Theater at 5th Avenue and High Street and other shops with nearly naked women dancing in the front windows, completing the sordid scene.

The neighborhood turned around in the 1980s with a commitment by the city and the business community to reinvest in the area. Columbus Police added more foot patrols to deter crime. The collaborative effort eventually turned the Short North into one of the most popular destinations in the city for food, arts, and nightlife.

The lighted Short North arches that span High Street in the district are the focal point of this popular area. The seventeen lighted steel arches run from Goodale Boulevard to Fifth Avenue.

5 NO SWEET TOOTH ON SUNDAY

Is it really illegal for shops to sell pastries and lemonade on Sundays?

Technically, yes. A Columbus City ordinance passed on June 20, 1853, prohibits grocery stores, saloons, confectionaries, or any establishment to sell pastries or lemonade on Sundays. The ordinance also prohibits the sale of wine, cider, and liquor, and though making an even trade of the Sunday-banned indulgences is not considered buying or selling, that is prohibited too.

The law is still on the books in Columbus, though more in concept than in practice.

Ironically, Sunday is one of the busiest days for pastry shops in the city as the suburbs expand and artisan bakeries become the preferred hangouts for coffee and sweets. Lemonade sales also boom on Sundays, especially during summer weekend festivals.

A DOZEN SCONES PLEASE

WHAT An obscure law still on the books banning the sale of sweets on Sundays

WHERE Throughout Columbus

COST Perhaps an extra workout in exchange for some specialty pastries

PRO TIP While the ordinance also banned liquor sales on Sundays, you can now legally purchase liquor during certain hours.

Some of Columbus's best artisan bakeries are found in German Village, Bexley, Clintonville, and at the North Market.

COFFEE
MACARON
$1.75

LEMON POPPY SE
MACARON

A selection of macarons available every day, but especially on Sundays.

In the mid-1800s violators of the law were subject to a fine of at least $10, but no more than $50, for each offense. The key enforcers of the law included the marshal of the city of Columbus and the captain of the night watch, positions that no longer exist. This could explain why the law lost its grip over the past 170 years. Thanks to the lax enforcement of the anti-pastry-on-Sunday ordinance, Columbus residents and visitors can enjoy more indulgent weekends in the city.

COLUMBUS DISPATCH NEWS TICKER

Where can I get the day's headlines while sitting in traffic?

For decades, it was impossible to drive along Third Street in downtown Columbus without getting a dose of the day's headlines from the scrolling news ticker on the former *Columbus Dispatch* building while waiting at a stoplight. Though the ticker's future is uncertain with the historic building under new ownership, it is a beloved part of the downtown scene.

Long before digital scrolling screens and LED lights, the *Columbus Dispatch* kept citizens abreast of the headlines even though it meant using everything but duct tape to display breaking news. In the early days before the modern downtown news ticker, the *Dispatch* used an old-school version called an electrograph. The device, developed circa 1917, was a jumbo-size screen that resembled a baseball stadium scoreboard. The electrograph, known as the "Dispatch Bulletin," kept the public informed about the events unfolding during World War I.

What is more impressive than the size of the ticker by today's standards is the genius required to operate it. The mechanics involved a typewriter hooked to electric lights on top of the building. Although the method sounds

---

Always on the cutting edge of news technology, the Columbus Dispatch was the first newspaper in America to go online, in 1980.

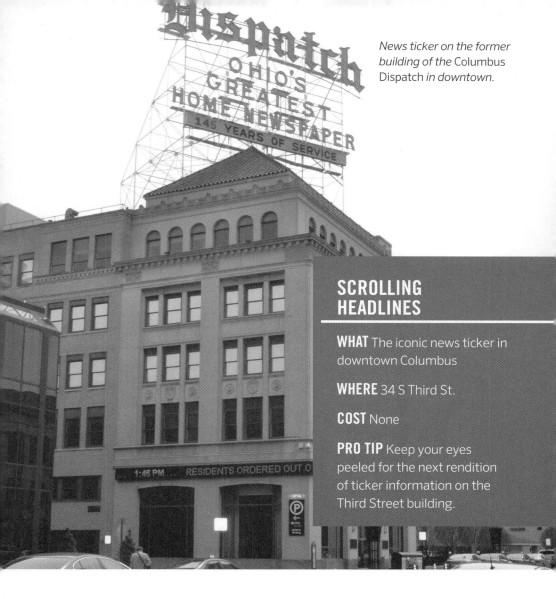

News ticker on the former building of the Columbus Dispatch *in downtown.*

SCROLLING HEADLINES

WHAT The iconic news ticker in downtown Columbus

WHERE 34 S Third St.

COST None

PRO TIP Keep your eyes peeled for the next rendition of ticker information on the Third Street building.

cumbersome and archaic, it was considered the forefront of technology for the early 1900s.

Times have changed quite a bit for the company and the news ticker. The *Daily Dispatch* was launched as an afternoon newspaper in 1871, starting a 110-year run in Columbus under the Wolfe family ownership. The paper changed hands in 2015 and the physical newsroom moved out of the Third Street building paving the way for a new era for the ticker in downtown Columbus.

WORLD'S FIRST JUNIOR HIGH SCHOOL

What is the big deal about this junior high school?

Junior high schools are an educational rite of passage in almost every community across the United States. Most cater to sixth through eighth graders or seventh through ninth graders. Ground zero for this transitional period of life, more casually referred to as middle school, started in Columbus at Indianola Junior High School.

The first incarnation of Indianola Junior High School opened in 1909 at Indianola and 16th Avenues. It did not take long for the novel idea to gain popularity, especially during the increase in population growth through the 1920s. The school quickly filled beyond capacity, requiring students to attend class in temporary spaces on the schoolyard.

The city responded by building additional middle schools, and Indianola Junior High moved into a bigger building on East 19th Avenue, where it stands today. The building still looks much like it did on opening day in 1929, featuring original architecture and stonework on the outside and wood trim inside.

The concept of a junior high school started in Columbus as a brainstorm between the Ohio State University President William Oxley Thompson and the Columbus Public Schools Superintendent Jacob Shawan. It evolved from concerns

---

Indianola Junior High School is listed on the Columbus Register of Historic Properties and the National Register of Historic Places.

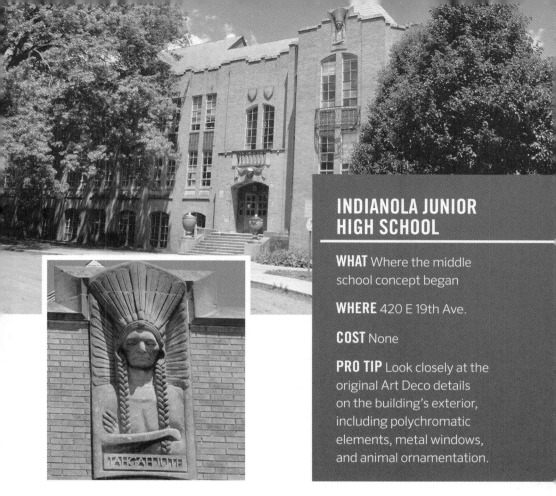

INDIANOLA JUNIOR HIGH SCHOOL

WHAT Where the middle school concept began

WHERE 420 E 19th Ave.

COST None

PRO TIP Look closely at the original Art Deco details on the building's exterior, including polychromatic elements, metal windows, and animal ornamentation.

Top: The second Indianola Junior High School.

Inset: The historic Indianola Middle School building has much of the original 1929 architecture.

about children leaving school to work after the eighth grade in the years before WWI. The result was a three-year middle school curriculum designed to decrease the dropout rates by easing the transition into high school.

As a testing ground for the middle school concept, school districts nationwide kept a close eye on this new idea. Little did anyone expect that this concept would transform the nation's educational system.

Indianola Middle School recently ceased operations as a working school, and it is on a list of properties for sale by the Columbus Public Schools.

15

⁸ WHERE THE INSANE ARE FORGOTTEN

Who would look for a place like this?

The answer is likely no one, and perhaps that is the point. The State of Ohio Asylum for the Insane Cemetery is tucked away at the end of a small dirt path located behind the Columbus Police heliport in a desolate industrial park. The understated iron gate entrance guards the nameless, faceless, forgotten patients from the old Columbus Mental Health Hospital.

OHIO INSANE ASYLUM CEMETERY

WHAT The final resting place for Ohio's forgotten mentally ill

WHERE Near McKinley Ave. and Harper Rd.

COST Free

PRO TIP The cemetery is very secluded so it is not advisable to go alone.

The grave markers for the deceased are the size of bricks marked with an "M" for male or "F" for female along with a patient number. Blades of grass in an open field disguise the rows of markers, secluding the patients the same way in death as they were in life. A stroll to the back of the grounds slowly reveals one row after another. In all, more than eight hundred markers consume the area that from the entrance looks like an empty field.

But this is not the most curious or stunning find in the cemetery.

More than one hundred patients died in any given year at the crowded State of Ohio Asylum for the Insane and were buried in its cemetery.

16

Several rows of marked headstones are the exception in the Ohio Insane Asylum Cemetery, as most are only marked by patient numbers.

Inset: A grave marker for a female patient, identified by "F," and another identified only as "Specimens" in the Ohio Insane Asylum Cemetery.

Hidden among a small section of mainstream headstones inside the gate is a find that triggers a bit of tingling in the spine. One marker in the middle of the others just says "specimens."

Perhaps it is the plural attribution that makes this discovery uncomfortable or the thought of what these asylum patients endured during a time when lobotomies and electroconvulsive therapies were common methods of treatment. Either way, it is impossible not to stare at the stone and ponder the possibilities.

The Ohio Lunatic Asylum on East Broad Street in the Hilltop opened its doors at more than double its capacity, with 330 patients, in 1838. After expansions and recovery from a devastating fire, the facility housed nearly 3,000 patients in 1935. A growing demand at the asylum over the next twenty years resulted in a staggering 14,000 patients by 1955.

9 TIGERS AREN'T JUST AT THE ZOO

Where are exotic animals held that are seized from private owners?

Appearances can be deceiving, especially at the Ohio Department of Agriculture campus on Main Street in Reynoldsburg. Behind the gates protecting the complex is a twenty-thousand-square-foot facility with more than one hundred exotic animals confiscated from private owners in Ohio. The animals include bears, tigers, lions, alligators, cougars, snakes, leopards, crocodiles, wolves, servals, and even an occasional liger.

The facility is a result of the Ohio Dangerous Wild Animal Act, a controversial law signed in June 2012 by Governor John Kasich. It bans private ownership of certain exotic animals in the state.

The law and the controversy that still lingers over it stem from a 2011 incident in Zanesville, where fifty-six exotic animals escaped from a private farm. Authorities were forced to kill forty-nine of the Bengal tigers, bears, and lions that were found near homes and highways in Muskingum County.

The backlash from the nationally publicized incident spurred tighter regulations on exotic animal ownership in Ohio. The $2.9 million Dangerous Wild Animal Temporary

---

The Dangerous Wild Animal Temporary Holding Facility is only designed to hold seized animals until they are placed in accredited sanctuaries in other states.

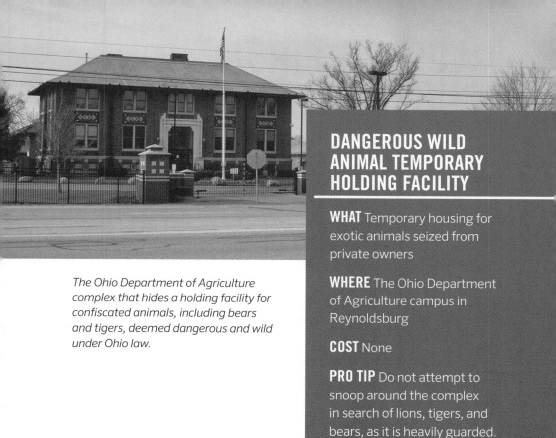

The Ohio Department of Agriculture complex that hides a holding facility for confiscated animals, including bears and tigers, deemed dangerous and wild under Ohio law.

DANGEROUS WILD ANIMAL TEMPORARY HOLDING FACILITY

WHAT Temporary housing for exotic animals seized from private owners

WHERE The Ohio Department of Agriculture campus in Reynoldsburg

COST None

PRO TIP Do not attempt to snoop around the complex in search of lions, tigers, and bears, as it is heavily guarded.

Holding Facility was built to help enforce the law. The building can hold twenty-seven large animals (such as bears) and has additional enclosures for alligators, primates, and snakes.

Although the facility is unassuming from the exterior and sits adjacent to a residential neighborhood, the chance of getting anywhere near it is slim, and the chance of going inside is nil. The containment facility is secured with a twelve-foot electric fence topped with barbed wire. Animals are housed within double or triple enclosures, and 360° cameras have eyes monitoring seventeen locations in and around the facility 24/7.

Although the new addition to the Ohio Department of Agriculture complex is off limits to public viewing, there is no doubt intrigue while driving by, just knowing about the virtual zoo inside.

WORLD'S FIRST SUBURBAN STRIP MALL

How did Columbus change the norm of neighborhood shopping?

The Town & Country Shopping Center on East Broad Street has undergone a number of face-lifts over the years, but when it was built, it set the standard for shopping at suburban strip malls across the United States.

As city dwellers started migrating to the suburbs in the 1950s as a result of the development of interstates, retailers had to find new ways to attract consumers. Shopping became less of a necessity and more of a convenience. Retailers responded by centralizing various types of businesses into one location.

Town & Country was the first such place to cater to the idea of one-stop shopping for food, clothing, and essentials like banks and restaurants.

It did not take long for the suburban shopping experience to catch on in other cities. By the late 1900s, similar concept-shopping centers developed in every major city in Ohio, and it set the bar for neighborhood shopping across the country.

The Town & Country Shopping Center, which opened in 1949, has stood the test of time even as large indoor malls began replacing suburban strip malls. Town & Country is a Columbus cornerstone, and although the tenants have changed a bit over the decades, it will always be the original.

The Town & Country Shopping Center housed the first branch location of a JCPenney's department store.

Stores at the Town & Country Shopping Center range from restaurants to banks.

Inset: Town & Country Shopping Center in northeast Columbus.

TOWN & COUNTY SHOPPING CENTER

WHAT The first strip mall to offer centralized shopping

WHERE 3772 E Broad St.

COST None to window shop

PRO TIP The concept of adding entertainment venues within the suburban shopping experience also started in Columbus.

Today Town & Country Shopping Center is an open-air strip mall with several dozen shops and restaurants, a post office, fitness center, and nail and beauty services.

11 "CARMEN OHIO" LYRICS

Wait, there is more than one verse?

Football Saturdays in the fall are sacred in Columbus. That is when thousands of OSU football fans pack into the Ohio Stadium to cheer on the Buckeyes and share an emotional moment singing "Carmen Ohio." There are several versions of the alma mater, but most fans do not know the complete one.

A freshman by the name of Fred Cornell wrote "Carmen Ohio" in 1902 at the request of the Men's Glee Club. Although only the first verse gets the spotlight at football games and in tributes to OSU, there are actually three verses.

A 1902 *Ohio State Lantern* article shares the full version of "Carmen Ohio," which might be the last time anyone has seen the final two verses.

CARMEN OHIO

WHAT The most beloved song at The Ohio State University

WHERE OSU stadium or anywhere in Columbus that fans break out in spontaneous song

COST None

PRO TIP If you are new to Columbus or do not know the words to "Carmen Ohio," learn the first verse and you will instantly feel like a native.

"Carmen Ohio" song lyrics printed in a 1906 newspaper article in the Ohio State Lantern. *Credit: OSU Libraries University Archives.*

Carmen Ohio

Oh come let's sing Ohio's praise
And songs to Alma Mater raise
While our hearts rebounding thrill
With joy which death alone can still
Summer's heat or winter's cold
The seasons pass the years will roll
Time and change will surely (truly) show
How firm thy friendship . . . OHIO!

These jolly days of priceless worth
By far the gladdest days on earth
Soon will pass and we not know
How dearly we love Ohio
We should strive to keep thy name
Of fair repute and spotless fame
So in college halls we'll grow
And love thee better . . . OHIO!

Though age may dim our mem'ry's store
We'll think of happy days of yore
True to friend and frank to foe
As sturdy sons of Ohio
If on seas of care we roll
Neath blackened sky or barren shoal
Thoughts of thee bid darkness go
Dear Alma Mater...OHIO!

Whether the Buckeyes win or lose, OSU fans can rejoice in knowing that there is more of "Carmen Ohio" to love.

"Carmen Ohio" was adapted from the tune of "Spanish Hymn" and is a beloved traditional anthem that often echoes throughout the stadium and the city.

<u>12</u> HOME OF THE SLIDER

One of the original "to go" bags developed by White Castle

How can White Castle® fanatics get a sneak peek behind the scenes?

White Castle, home of "the slider," is headquartered in Columbus and is an institution in the city. A taste of the famous tiny square burger with onions and a pickle is a rite of passage for Columbusites.

While there are several White Castle restaurants in Columbus harboring a taste that has a cult following across the country, the headquarters, located on Goodale Street, hides something else that most fans, dubbed "cravers," do not know.

White Castle's command central does not offer public tours, but they will grant a tour of the headquarters and maybe even a slider meal to fans who call and ask nicely. Inside the lobby are showcases filled with White Castle memorabilia. On display are some of the earliest versions of the original china coffee mugs and plates used in the restaurants, as well as one of the primitive renditions of the slider hamburger box.

WHITE CASTLE HEADQUARTERS

WHAT A permitted snoop behind the Castle walls

WHERE 555 W Goodale St.

COST Polite words and a good attitude

PRO TIP White Castle originally served burgers and coffee on fine china but stopped when dinnerware began disappearing.

There are 420 White Castle restaurants in the United States, and you can still buy the original slider for under $1.00.

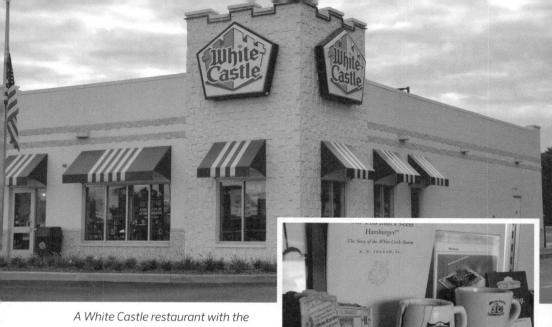

A White Castle restaurant with the iconic architecture.

Inset: China coffee cups and original burger boxes among the memorabilia on display at the White Castle headquarters.

Catch a rare glimpse of historic photos and learn the details about White Castle's many "firsts" in the fast food industry. The company was the first hamburger chain that used and revolutionized restaurant cleanliness with stainless steel counters. They were also one of the first fast food restaurants to offer to-go bags.

White Castle opened in 1921 in Wichita, Kansas, selling five-cent hamburgers and introducing the concept of a fast food burger. The small patty is famous for its five equally spaced holes that ensure even distribution of heat. Within a decade the company developed the cardboard carton for the hamburgers, promoting take-out with the slogan "Buy 'em by the Sack." By 1963 White Castle had sold more than two billion hamburgers.

White Castle moved its headquarters to Columbus, Ohio, in 1934, where its humble building stands today.

It is nice to know that despite the near century-long success of this family-owned business, it still pays to "ask nicely."

White Castle is a registered trademark of White Castle Management Company.

NINETEENTH-CENTURY AMUSEMENTS

What did fun look like in the early days of Columbus?

If the ground beneath the Olentangy Village Apartments in Clintonville could spill secrets, there would be plenty to share. The once-thriving Olentangy Amusement Park brought that neighborhood to life in the late 1800s. What started as a picnic park called The Villa in 1893, with swimming and boating on the Olentangy River, evolved into a popular entertainment destination.

In its heyday (1910-1920), the Olentangy Amusement Park featured a dance pavilion, zoo, Japanese Garden and Tea House, roller coasters, and a performance theater that attracted top vaudeville, opera, and minstrel acts. An outdoor pavilion hosted amateur night boxing and wrestling, which attracted a younger crowd. Families were drawn to the park's water amusements with popular rides like Shoot-the-Chutes, an old-school version of the splashing water log ride. It also featured the world's largest swimming pool, with several tons of sand trucked in from New Jersey—complete with seashells—to create an oceanside experience.

By the 1930s, the Great Depression and expanding entertainment options in Columbus took a toll on park attendance. The Olentangy Amusement Park closed in 1937 to make way for development of the Olentangy Village apartments that are still there today.

As many as forty thousand visitors passed through the Olentangy Amusement Park gates on any given day in the early 1900s.

OLENTANGY AMUSEMENT PARK

WHAT Remnants of the early amusement park years in Columbus

WHERE Near Olentangy Village Apartments off High Street and the curve of North Street

COST None

PRO TIP For the truly adventurous looking for more park remnants along the Olentangy River, the easiest access is from the bridge on Ackerman Road. Those finds are not as accessible and require more diligent and careful exploration.

Top: Original zookeeper's quarters at Olentangy Park now houses apartments.

Above: Olentangy Village Apartments on the grounds of what used to be Olentangy Park.

While any semblance of an amusement park is gone, there are still scattered remnants of what was once the largest amusement park in the United States. Just south of the Olentangy Village Apartments on North Street is the original wrought iron fence from the park. Just beyond the sharp curve on the same street is an original stone building that served as the zookeeper's quarters and park office.

More hidden remnants of Olentangy Park sit along the banks of the Olentangy River near Ackerman Road, including foundations of walking bridges and steps from the old park theater.

14 THE BEST OPEN-AIR VIEW OF COLUMBUS

Where is the best panoramic view of downtown Columbus?

Arguably the best view of downtown Columbus from every direction is in a place that almost no one knows even exists. An enclosed observation deck in The James A. Rhodes State Office Tower is open to the public, but because no one expects this kind of tourist attraction in a guarded government building, the 40th floor in the tower is the best kept secret in Columbus.

As the tallest skyscraper in the capital city at 629 feet, the Rhodes State Office Tower houses mostly government offices and remains under tight security. With a visitor badge issued by the front desk security guard, however, the general public is allowed access to the 40th floor for an unforgettable vista of the expanding downtown landscape.

RHODES STATE OFFICE TOWER OBSERVATORY DECK

WHAT A memorable aerial view of downtown Columbus

WHERE 30 E Broad St.

COST None

PRO TIP The Rhodes State Office Tower is a high-security building, so you will need to check in with photo identification at the security desk.

The 41-story Rhodes State Office Tower is named after James A. Rhodes, who served four terms as Ohio's governor in the 1960s and 1970s.

One of the panoramic views of the Columbus city skyline from the Rhodes State Office Tower observation deck.

Inset: Rhodes State Office Tower building in downtown Columbus.

Hallways that span the full perimeter of the building on the north, south, east, and west sides allow visitors uninterrupted views that expand far beyond the metro area on clear days. Signs posted in each hallway point out notable buildings and landmarks that visitors can identify in each direction.

The east-facing hallway has the added surprise of a large mural depicting symbols from the state of Ohio, like the large white trillium flower, buckeye tree, and white-tailed deer. Local muralist Mandi Caskey created the artwork to reflect the features that are unique to the state on a backdrop of Ohio's four seasons. The mural is an educational piece allowing visitors to seek and find the natural beauty of Ohio.

15 A STROLL DOWN MEMORY LANE

Where do tree-lined streets have extra meaning?

Take a stroll down Memory Lane on West North Broadway, or at least the remnants of it. This stretch of roadway decorated by a canopy of crabapple trees was known as Memory Lane in the 1940s, serving as a tribute to local soldiers who died in World War II.

Memorial stone dedicated to soldiers from Clintonville as part of the Memory Lane project. Credit: Roberta Hamper.

What originated as a tree-planting beautification project by the Clintonville Woman's Club in 1939 became a memorial effort after America joined WWII. A crabapple tree was planted for each soldier who died, and the tree was dedicated with a plaque that recognized the soldier's name, rank, and unit. Memory Lane served as the only memorial for many soldiers whose bodies were never returned home for a proper burial.

Trees were planted on the north and south sides of West North Broadway from Milton Avenue to Olentangy River Road and adorned with flags and flowers throughout the year by civic associations.

The one hundred soldier plaques that were relocated to Union Cemetery are only a fraction of the hundreds that originally lined Memory Lane.

Memory Lane memorial plates that are now located in Union Cemetery. Credit: Roberta Hamper.

The highway development project of State Route 315 in 1981 required removing much of Memory Lane and decades of history with it. The only portion left of the project is a few crabapple trees along the roadway that still beautify the area when in bloom.

The metal plates bearing the names of the deceased local servicemen were relocated to nearby Union Cemetery. Almost directly upon entering the cemetery at the top of the hill is the center-island memorial bearing all of the metal plates.

In recent years the Clintonville Historical Society has begun recreating Memory Lane. There are currently four gardens, each with a memorial monument. The most recent monument is *Cynthia's Compass,* a tribute to Clintonville's involvement in the Underground Railroad.

MEMORY LANE

WHAT A beautiful drive with special meaning

WHERE Crabapple trees are located along W North Broadway between Milton Ave. and Olentangy River Rd. Memory Lane memorial plates are located at Union Cemetery on Olentangy River Rd.

COST None

PRO TIP The best time to enjoy the beauty of the Memory Lane crabapple canopy is in the spring when the flowers are in bloom.

THE ORIGINAL MR. PEANUT

Where is the original Mr. Peanut still twirling his cane?

High above The Peanut Shoppe in downtown Columbus is a neon sign featuring one of America's most iconic brand mascots, Mr. Peanut. A mainstay in downtown Columbus for more than 81 years, Mr. Peanut still welcomes people who walk into the tiny store to get their daily fix of hot roasted nuts and candies.

The exterior Mr. Peanut hanging on the side of the building is the only original neon sign featuring Mr. Peanut still in public use from the 1930s. Owner Pat Stone knows of only two others in existence; they remain hidden in private collections.

The Planters mascot with his famed top hat, monocle, and cane is just one of several treasured items that remain from the original Planters Peanut Company store that opened in Columbus in 1936.

The original roasters still crank out fresh hot cashews, and vintage calibrated balance scales are still used to weigh

The original Mr. Peanut costume in the store is the one current owner Mike Stone wore in 1972 to promote the existing peanut shop at that time. He used the $1.50 per hour he made in those days to take his future wife on dates while they were in high school. The couple then bought the Peanut Shoppe in 1996.

Original peacut roasters still crank out
fresh nuts daily at the Peanut Shoppe.

THE PEANUT SHOPPE

WHAT Original peanut shop
and candy store in downtown
Columbus

WHERE 21 E State St.

COST The per-pound price
of your favorite nostalgic
candy, but breathing in the
indulgent smell of peanuts
and chocolate is free

PRO TIP When you walk
into the Peanut Shoppe, ask
"What's hot?" to find out the
daily selection of Spanish
peanuts, walnuts, cashews, or
hazelnuts that are currently
hot in the roaster.

the candy. The store showcases a collection of Mr. Peanut
memorabilia, including old jars, tins, and a roaster rider that
dates back to the early 1900s. The store's retro environment
adds to the enjoyment of the original candy favorites for sale,
like chocolate peanuts, spice drops, maple nuts goodies, and
peanut butter logs.

Most of the original Mr. Peanut signs and product
memorabilia, were destroyed in 1961 when Standard Brands
purchased the National Peanut Corporation. The new company
sent men with hammers to the company's three hundred retail
stores to destroy all of the promotional products. Negative
press put a halt to the mission just before the men arrived in
Columbus, which is why these salvaged items are some of the
only ones left in existence.

Mr. Peanut and his store have moved three times to different
locations in downtown Columbus but never more than a block
from the statehouse.

THE PAGODA MYSTERY

Why is there an Asian-style pagoda in downtown Columbus?

As Columbus's downtown development takes hold with a riverfront landscape, green space, and new skyscrapers, one building stands out with its curious Asian motif. It was unusual even its heyday in the late 1800s on West Broad Street.

The pagoda-style building, called Station 67, is the home of Columbus Firefighters Local 67 and can be rented out as space for events and weddings. It was originally a train depot for the Toledo and Ohio Central Railroad in 1895 and still features nineteenth-century marble floor tiles, original woodwork, and plaster cherubs on the arch walls.

Above: The historic T&OC railroad depot on Broad Street.

The depot ceased operations in 1930 when the New York Central Railroad purchased T&OC. While the depot architecture is admired, no one has been able to pinpoint exactly how or why it appears to imitate an Asian pagoda. One theory is that renowned Columbus architecture firm Yost & Packard designed the transportation hub after Swiss and French feudal architecture. Another theory is that the Japanese-influenced pagoda was intended to complement the three pagoda towers on the Macklin Hotel that once stood across the tracks.

Though the building is used for events, anyone can stop by to look inside the grand lobby of the train depot. The interior walls still vibrate from passing rail cars, and the

Left: Original ticket counter inside the T&OC train depot.

Right: Inside the historic train depot that looks the same as it did in the 1800s.

original ticket window in the lobby offers a glimpse into what daily life was like more than a century ago. An indentation on the floor beneath the ticket window reveals where passengers wore a groove in the floor while they stood swinging one foot on the ground waiting to complete a transaction.

Throughout the decades, the building survived fires, floods, and new owners. It served as the headquarters for the Volunteers of America for seventy-three years, housing the homeless in the courtyard before the Columbus Firefighters Union Local 67 purchased the building and gave it new purpose in 2007.

STATION 67

WHAT One of the most unusual looking buildings in Columbus

WHERE 379 W Broad St.

COST None

PRO TIP Station 67 is on the National Register of Historic Places.

The grand lobby of the depot was underwater during the deadly 1913 flood that killed 732 people and halted rail transportation in several states. A small plaque on the interior balcony staircase marks the flood level.

<u>18</u> SECRET MAZE BELOW CAMPUS

What elaborate network operates beneath the OSU campus?

Navigating the sprawling Ohio State University campus above ground is complex enough, but there is an even more elaborate maze below the surface. The 36,803 feet of steam and electric tunnels operating between campus buildings is

A view through the grate at McCracken Power Plant into the tunnels below.

an efficient way to operate and maintain utilities. To put the complexity of the network into proper perspective, it is important to understand that the nearly seven miles of tunnels are intertwined beneath 2.9 square miles of campus.

Some of the earliest steam tunnels beneath OSU were constructed in 1906 as a way to bring heating and lighting to university buildings. The tunnels proved necessary in order to provide utilities without digging up campus lawns. The tunnels range in size. Some are just large enough for a person to walk upright and others are barely passable to anything larger than a small animal.

Tunnel extensions over the years now provide utilities to more than one

The tunnel maze beneath OSU started at Brown Hall using labor from the Ohio Penitentiary for construction.

Location of the grate over the OSU tunnels behind the McCracken Power Plant.

OSU'S TUNNEL MAZE

WHAT A complex network of steam and electric tunnels beneath the OSU campus

WHERE The best view is from the McCracken Power Plant on Millikin Rd.

COST None

PRO TIP Do not attempt to access the tunnel system on your own, as it is illegal.

hundred campus buildings including electric, water, steam, and fiber optic cables. There are several entry points to the tunnels, but it is illegal and dangerous to attempt to access them. Security measures are also in place to prevent any curious exploration.

One of the best places to safely get a glimpse of the tunnels is behind the McCracken Power Plant on Millikin Road. The grated vent located midway along the building enables a safe view of the utility pipes and brick walls below that line the arched passageways.

Oftentimes OSU offers an authorized Things You Never Got to See Tour during spring commencement week.

¹⁹ POLYNESIAN MEMORIES AND MEMORABILIA

Are there any existing relics of the famed Kahiki Supper Club?

Columbus natives or residents of the city prior to the year 2000 remember the iconic Kahiki Supper Club. The restaurant was a sensory experience in every way. The commanding forty-foot-tall building with twenty-foot

flaming Moai statues at the door was designed to look like a Polynesian fighting boat. The entrance led guests into a dark Pacific Island tropical rainforest reminiscent of the opening scene of the television show *Fantasy Island*.

At the bar of The Grass Skirt Tiki Room, where much of the original drink glassware from the Kahiki Supper Club is on display.

The Kahiki Supper Club forever changed the Columbus dining experience when it opened on East Broad Street in 1961. Every element—from the extravagant and kitschy décor to the lighting and sound effects simulating an Easter Island rainstorm—teased the imagination. The famous Mai Tais and specialty drinks came with as much flare as the exotic Mystery Girl waitresses dressed in tribal regalia who delivered them.

The Kahiki company is now exclusively in the frozen food business, selling many favorites like the egg rolls that were popular at the iconic restaurant.

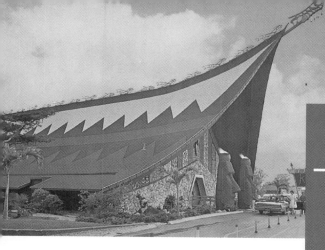

The original Kahiki Supper Club restaurant. Photo credit: Kahik.

GRASS SKIRT TIKI ROOM

WHAT Where you can find original Kahiki Supper Club glassware, memorabilia, and George the monkey fountain

WHERE 105 N Grant Ave.

COST Free to look at the kitschy décor, but the smoking drinks are worth the price of entertainment

PRO TIP To recreate the Kahiki experience, try a house specialty "Bowls for Sharing" cocktail like the Headhunter's Sangria. Add to it a flaming topper or smoking spirit and watch all eyes in the room follow the drink to your table.

The nostalgia and fondness for the Kahiki remains strong in Columbus. When the restaurant closed in 2000 and was subsequently demolished, no one really knew what happened to the relics.

It turns out, a small venue called the Grass Skirt Tiki Room in downtown Columbus acquired many of the most memorable pieces from the Kahiki restaurant. This restaurant seats approximately fifty people—not five hundred like the Kahiki—but the feeling is similar inside, with dim lighting and exotic décor mimicking a South Pacific island.

The intimate lounge has its own collection of quirky drink glasses, but many of the original Kahiki tiki glasses and menus are on display. The large George the monkey fountain that once guarded the Kahiki entrance now welcomes outdoor guests at the Grass Skirt Tiki Lounge. They even acquired and continue to serve some of the original drink recipes, like the Port Light Tiki Classic that was first served at the Kihiki in 1962.

20 WHEN OUTDOOR CONCERTS ROCKED COLUMBUS

Where was the prime concert venue in Columbus?

The existence of the Germain Amphitheater is immortalized as somewhat of a one-hit wonder when it comes to the longevity of entertainment venues in Columbus. It opened as Polaris Amphitheater on June 15, 1994, changing the live music scene. This was a first-of-its-kind outdoor concert venue for the city.

THE GERMAIN AMPHITHEATER

WHAT Once Columbus's largest outdoor concert venue

WHERE I-71 and Polaris Parkway near Westerville

COST None

PRO TIP The last concert, performed by Toby Keith, was September 16, 2007.

Eventually renamed the Germain Amphitheater, there were concerts almost every night of the week entertaining twenty thousand fans at a time. The amphitheater hosted major artists throughout the years, including Aerosmith, RUSH, Jimmy Buffet, Janet Jackson, and Toby Keith; benefit concerts like Farm Aid; and the rock festival Ozzfest.

The open-air concert experience achieved instant popularity with everyone except the neighbors who lived behind the venue. After years of controversy over the noise, the cost of doing business, and rising real-estate prices, the amphitheater closed after the 2007 season. The lot sat empty while vandals looted and destroyed what was left of Columbus concert memories until it was demolished in 2012.

There is new life on the property in the form of an IKEA store, but evidence of the old amphitheater is still visible. Just beyond the store on IKEA Way is the original parking

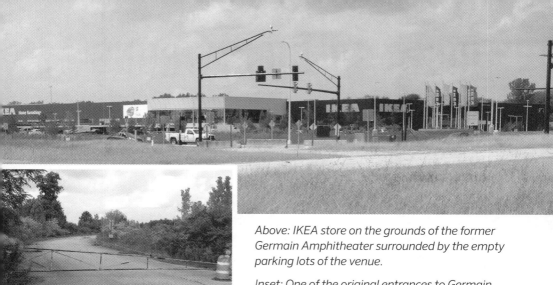

Above: IKEA store on the grounds of the former Germain Amphitheater surrounded by the empty parking lots of the venue.

Inset: One of the original entrances to Germain Amphitheater, now closed off and abandoned.

lot and wooden amphitheater fencing that is now overgrown with weeds. Both are visible from the roadway. That is the only way to observe them, as there is no trespassing allowed on the property.

Another way to view amphitheater yesteryear is from the original second entrance to the amphitheater parking lot off Polaris Parkway. The dead-end roadway is still walkable up to a gate. There is no legal access, but directional signs once used to point departing concert-goers to the highway still stand and are visible from the gate.

Even a drive-by look at the former land of Germain Amphitheater instills a sense of nostalgia. The Columbus music scene has not been the same since.

The 1997 Ozzfest concert at the Germain Amphitheater turned into a near riot, with fans smashing glass on the stage, starting fires, overturning cars, and destroying box office windows.

RIGHT SOLDIER, WRONG NAME

How was a prominent decorated soldier buried under the wrong name?

The second headstone for Stanislaus Roy with his first name still spelled incorrectly. Credit: Sandy Holladay

Sorting out the story behind Congressional Medal of Honor recipient Stanislaus Roy, buried in Green Lawn Cemetery under the wrong name for ninety years, is like engaging in a round of "Who's on First?"

The decorated soldier's body was lost among the famous graves in Columbus's largest cemetery for nearly a century. U.S. Army Sergeant Stanislaus Roy earned the Congressional Medal of Honor during the Battle of Little Bighorn, also called Custer's Last Stand, on June 25, 1876. He earned the honor for putting his life in danger by crossing enemy fire to collect water for wounded soldiers from a ravine. His heroic efforts serving the U.S. Army in Company A, 7th Calvary, saved several lives when most of his unit was killed.

The sergeant was buried in Green Lawn Cemetery under the name of Roy Stanislas after his death on February 10, 1913, at the age of sixty-six. Because his name was engraved last name first and misspelled ("Stanislas" instead of "Stanislaus") on his grave marker, no one could find him.

How could this a mix-up happen to a prominent soldier involved in such a significant battle in U.S. history? And why is it that no one noticed for more than ninety years?

The reason is that no one was looking for Stanislaus Roy until a researcher uncovered the drastic mistake in the 1990s while trying to find his grave. After the discovery, the

WHAT Congressional Medal of Honor recipient buried under the wrong name for ninety years

WHERE Green Lawn Cemetery, Post Cemetery, Section 51, Plot A, Space 183

COST None

PRO TIP There are thirty miles of roads in the cemetery, so stop in the cemetery office for a detailed map to the grave plot.

The grave of Stanislaus Roy is marked with a "section under renovation" sign as it awaits a third corrected headstone.

sergeant received a new headstone with his name in the right order, but unfortunately that is not the end of the story. His first name was still spelled incorrectly, missing the letter "u."

Upon a recent visit to the gravesite, I found the second headstone is now gone and replaced with a temporary "section under renovation" marker. Perhaps Stanislaus Roy is getting a third—and finally correct—headstone after 140 years.

Sergeant Stanislaus Roy was one of twenty-four soldiers in the 7th Calvary who earned the Congressional Medal of Honor during the Battle of Little Bighorn when General George Custer's unit attacked Native American Lakota Sioux and Northern Cheyenne Indians at the Little Big Horn River.

22

THE NARROWING ROAD

Why does High Street appear to narrow in the Short North?

The stretch of High Street near the Short North is a constant hub of activity, so it is unlikely that anyone even notices that some sections of the corridor are wider than the rest.

The changing width of High Street is due to a widening project from the 1920s that never came to fruition. The project folded prematurely but not before some sections were widened, some not, and some sections widened then narrowed again with street and building modifications. The clarification on dates and numbers has even the history experts and city engineers cross-eyed.

Discussions about widening High Street began in 1885 when the city wanted to add another streetcar track. The section of High Street north of the train depot was sixty-feet wide. In order to add a second track for streetcars and still have room for automobiles and pedestrian traffic, considerable alterations had to be made to existing structures along High Street.

The city wanted to add ten feet on each side of High Street from Spruce to Buttles and eighteen feet from Buttles to Fifth Avenue. In order to do that, commercial buildings either had to be moved back or have their façades eliminated. Some businesses used it as an opportunity to renovate their storefronts with modern

THE GREYSTONE BUILDING

WHAT One of many businesses along High Street that shaved off its façade to accommodate a widening project that was never completed

WHERE 815 N High St.

COST None

PRO TIP The Greystone Building currently houses upper apartments with street-front retail space.

The Greystone Building was one of many businesses that removed a twelve-foot section of its façade to accommodate the widening of High Street in 1922.

architecture but for others like the Greystone Building it required an extreme and expensive effort.

Just as construction was completed on the Greystone Building in 1922, the owners had to remove a twelve-foot section from each of the north and south sides. Less than a year later, when the city abandoned the project, the owners carefully reattached the 4.5-story façade using mules to move the massive stone sections one inch at a time. Surprisingly, however, examining the present-day building there is no sign of the dramatic reattachment.

The cost to remove and reattach the façade of the Greystone Building to accommodate the widening of High Street was more than the entire cost of construction of the original building.

SUPREME JUSTICE

Where can I find the world's largest gavel in Columbus?

It is not difficult to spot the larger-than-life stainless steel gavel outside of the Thomas J. Moyer Ohio Judicial Center on South Front Street. The thirty-one-foot-long, seven-thousand-pound judicial mallet sits in the south reflecting pool outside of the Ohio State Supreme Court on the Scioto riverfront.

Although the gavel is said to be the world's largest, it was originally supposed to be twice the size. Artist Andrew Scott crafted his metal sculpture, entitled *Gavel,* in 2008 to represent the judicial authority of the Ohio State Supreme Court, which meets in the building behind the plaza. Due to the price of steel at the time, Scott was forced to reduce the size of the sculpture. It is a fitting piece to enhance the landscape of the Ohio Judicial Center that was built in 1933 and renovated in 2001.

OHIO JUDICIAL CENTER

WHAT The world's largest gavel

WHERE 65 S Front St.

COST None

PRO TIP One of the best spots for a selfie in downtown Columbus

---

Visitors to the Ohio Judicial Center can take a free, forty-five-minute, volunteer-led tour of the artwork in the building and are free to sit in the courtroom gallery to listen to any Supreme Court proceedings in session.

The plaza that surrounds the gavel at the Ohio Judiciary Center is a popular lunch spot and sitting area for downtown workers. Credit: The Supreme Court of Ohio.

Inset: The late Chief Justice of the Ohio Supreme Court Thomas J. Moyer and artist Andrew F. Scott, who designed the large gavel sculpture. Credit: The Supreme Court of Ohio.

The large gavel is just one piece of the Judicial Center's extensive collection of contemporary artwork inside and outside of the building. There are sixty-one murals and mosaics representing important milestones in Ohio history, along with sculptures and paintings by Ohio artists.

To counterbalance the sculpture *Gavel,* which sits in the south reflecting pool, there is an equally impressive visual in the north reflecting pool. In that pool, ten words representing the justice system are carved in the granite just below the water. The inscription reads: "wisdom, peace, honor, compassion, integrity, equity, truth, reason, justice, and honesty."

What are the origins of the famous buckeye candy in Columbus?

Columbus may be the home of the Buckeyes, as in the Ohio State University football Buckeyes, but it is also the birthplace of the tiny chocolate-covered peanut butter candies of the same name. The addicting buckeye candies are designed to look like the nut of the buckeye tree, the state tree of Ohio.

The buckeye confection, so representative of the Buckeye State and found in nearly every gift shop, got its start in Columbus as a cookie called the "hetuck."

A woman named Gloria Hoover won the blue ribbon at the Ohio State Fair in 1965 for her grandmother's unnamed anise seed sugar cookie recipe in the "Best Rolled Cookies" category. The cookies ended up winning the prized rosette for the best cookies at the fair that year, and Hoover went home with a recipe in demand.

Overwhelmed with requests for the cookie, Hoover started a small baking company and gave the cookie a more formal name, the hetuck, which is the Native American word for buckeye. The hetuck evolved into what is now known as the candy buckeye. By 1968, Hoover's buckeye endeavor took on a life of its own, forcing her to expand operations and travel to promote the small, delicious candies.

THE CANDY BUCKEYE

WHAT The famed peanut butter and chocolate confection that started in Columbus

WHERE Most gift shops and candy stores in Columbus

COST It depends on how many you buy

PRO TIP Do not plan on eating just one.

Buckeye candy is on prominent displays in Anthony-Thomas candy stores.

Inset: Popular Buckeyes candy sold by Anthony-Thomas candy shops in Columbus

The hetucks were originally packaged and marketed in small metal tins. While you can still find buckeyes sold in metal tins, most of them now are sold in boxes or fresh off the tray at Anthony-Thomas candy stores.

The buckeye candies as we know them today were given as gifts to governors, congressmen, and even President Richard Nixon during a speech in Newark, Ohio, in 1966 before they became a cult classic on their own.

BRUSHSTROKES IN FLIGHT

What is Columbus's most expensive and controversial piece of art?

Mention *Brushstrokes in Flight* around town and anyone who has been here long enough is likely to have an emphatic reaction of either delight or disdain. Never has there been a more controversial, despised, or expensive piece of artwork in Columbus than the thirty-foot-tall *Brushstrokes in Flight* sculpture at the John Glenn Columbus International Airport.

The $150,000 sculpture, designed by Roy Lichtenstein, made its first public appearance on March 14, 1984, permanently influencing the public art conversation in Columbus. The red, yellow, and blue sculpture was part of a marketing campaign for "Discover Columbus" that complemented versions of the logo stamped on stationery and promotional products for the city.

Lichtenstein designed the sculpture to represent a "sense of flight" to fit the airport environment and welcome visitors to the capital city. Columbusites, angry over the cost of what they considered an unsightly embarrassment for the city, never warmed to it.

In 1988, Mayor Dana Rinehart offered to gift *Brushstrokes in Flight* to the city of Genoa, Italy, as a thank you for the gift of the Christopher Columbus statue in 1955 that remains outside of City Hall. The resulting uproar in the Columbus arts community halted the plan.

The Brushstrokes in Flight *art installation stands proudly in the atrium of John Glenn International Airport to welcome visitors to the city.*

Perhaps that is why the problematic statue has been relocated several times. It was moved from a remote courtyard at the airport to an area near the parking lots, before finally getting a more prominent spot inside the terminal in 1998 as the centerpiece of the atrium.

Three decades have done little to quell the polarizing opinions over *Brushstrokes in Flight,* even though it was designed by one of the most influential contemporary artists of the late twentieth century.

BRUSHSTROKES IN FLIGHT

WHAT The most controversial piece of artwork in Columbus

WHERE John Glenn Columbus International Airport

COST None

PRO TIP The sculpture's artist, Roy Lichtenstein, had strong ties to the Columbus community as an Ohio State University alumnus. He died in 1997.

26

DOWNTOWN TELEVISION

What happened to Columbus's first and only live downtown television studio?

The concept of a live television studio at Columbus's bustling intersection at Broad and High Streets downtown was a novel idea that was, unfortunately, short-lived. WCMH-TV (NBC4) launched *NBC4 on the Square* in 2008 with much fanfare, broadcasting the first live morning and noon newscasts from the heart of downtown.

The concept was modeled after the NBC *Today Show* out of New York, with anchors taking the news to the streets and talking to locals about current events during sidewalk interviews. The Ohio Statehouse as the backdrop for the newscasts added a sense of immediacy to the live broadcasts.

With only two news anchors, a weather man, an engineer, and two robotic cameras, NBC4 pulled off one of the most creative and exciting ventures in Columbus television history.

The downtown studio enticed a new kind of audience in Columbus television.

Tall glass studio windows allowed the passing public a front row seat, and sometimes an on-camera cameo during live news broadcasts. Multi-level digital marquees on the outside corner of the building flashed news updates, weather conditions, and promotions for news personalities. The million-dollar condos above the studio added additional excitement to the booming downtown development.

News anchor concerns about safety led to the installation of "bullet resistant" glass on the windows facing Broad Street.

Location of the former NBC4 on the Square downtown studio that now sits as empty space for lease.

Inset: Anietra Hamper anchors the morning newscast at NBC4 on the Square during a live broadcast in downtown Columbus.

NBC4 ON THE SQUARE DOWNTOWN STUDIO

WHAT A short-lived but highly publicized downtown television studio

WHERE The corner of Broad St. and High St.

COST None

PRO TIP *Secret Columbus* author Anietra Hamper was the principal news anchor during the inception of *NBC4 on the Square* for the morning and noon newscasts.

The downtown studio folded in 2011 after only a three-year run when a lease agreement on the building fell through. While the flashy digital marquee still operates on the outside corner at Broad and High Streets, the news anchors and cameras for NBC4 moved back to WCMH's main studio on Olentangy River Road. The downtown studio was parceled out into storefronts and has remained mostly vacant.

Today, there is little evidence beyond the bullet-resistant glass studio windows to suggest it ever existed.

27

OUT OF PLACE

Why does an oddly shaped building mingle with its symmetrical neighbors in downtown Columbus?

This is a question that people still ask today about the Flatiron Building that has stood proudly facing North Fourth Street since 1914. The wedge-shaped building is an anomaly among the towering, traditional square and rectangular buildings in downtown Columbus. While a number of other U.S. cities, including Pittsburgh and Atlanta, feature replicas of the famous Flatiron Building in New York, the Columbus version is unique in that its triangular format was not built on land of the same shape.

The short answer to the question is that rich developers can pretty much do anything for the right price and care little about "fitting in."

The more detailed answer lies in the imagination of a Columbus entrepreneur named Herbert Aloysius Higgins, who wanted to impress the locals in the early 1900s with something creative.

His creativity led to the conception of the Flatiron Building, which would be as eclectic in its use as in its design. The building is only eight feet wide on the narrowest side and four stories tall. The façade faces three directions and can be seen from Locust Street, Lazelle Street, North Fourth Street, and Nationwide Boulevard.

The Flatiron name for wedge-shaped buildings is derived from the resemblance they have to the cast-iron appliance that is used to press clothing.

FLATIRON BAR AND DINER

WHAT The oddest shaped building you will see in downtown Columbus

WHERE 129 E Nationwide Blvd.

COST Nothing to look and cheap to eat

PRO TIP A stone located on the top of the building is inscribed with "H.A. Higgins 1914."

The Flatiron Bar and Diner in downtown Columbus adds historic charm along Nationwide Boulevard.

The original building housed a saloon, grocery store, and apartments. Its location near the railroad tracks made it a regular stop for circus employees before they boarded the train to the next city. During prohibition, the taproom became a restaurant and a reliable spot for a quick meal and neighborly conversation.

Today, the Flatiron Bar and Diner is a novelty place for happy hour, especially for downtown workers. The old-school charm of the eye-catching building adds a bit of personality to the Arena District. Patrons appreciate the bygone-era feel, and the saloon-style interior makes for a unique outing among the trendy downtown establishments.

As it turns out, Herbert Aloysius Higgins was not just an entrepreneur, but a marketing visionary.

<u>28</u> THE CAREFUL FLOW OF WASTE

How did experiments launch Columbus as an innovator in wastewater treatment?

Wastewater treatment is not a hot topic at cocktail parties, but kudos to the originators of this ingenious idea who, through experimentation, figured out a way to keep city water safe. Columbus was one of the first cities in the country to establish a wastewater treatment plant, in the late 1800s, developing a model that other cities would eventually follow.

Columbus currently operates two wastewater treatment plants: the Jackson Pike plant and the Southerly plant.

Because residents relied only on wells and cisterns for water in the 1800s, hundreds of people died during cholera

COLUMBUS WASTEWATER TREATMENT PLANTS

WHAT The silent clean water saviors in Columbus

WHERE Jackson Pike (2104 Jackson Pike), and Southerly (6977 S High St.)

COST None

PRO TIP The two plants in Columbus can treat more than 200 million gallons of water per day.

The Columbus wastewater system that started with seventy miles of pipes in 1871 now consists of nearly twenty-eight hundred miles of sanitary sewers collecting domestic and industrial waste throughout the city.

Water treatment operations at the Jackson Pike facility in Columbus. Credit: The City of Columbus.

outbreaks between 1833 and 1850. The tipping point came after a devastating fire in 1868 at the Central Asylum for the Insane that killed seven people. The fire department had an inadequate water supply to slow the inferno. The city's water problem was compounded by pollution coming from human and animal waste. These events led the city to get serious about the need for clean water and ample access to it.

The best solution at the time was to build a simple pumping station that could supply clean water into Columbus homes by 1871. Three decades of population growth made it necessary to find a more suitable solution. A series of experiments got underway in 1903 to analyze drinking and wastewater and with the world watching the project became internationally known as "The Columbus Experiment."

The experiments resulted in never-before tried methods of combining filtration and water softening systems forever changing the way Columbus and the cities monitoring the progress of the experiments looked at wastewater treatment. The cutting edge methods were implemented in 1908 with a new facility to replace the original antiquated system. The Scioto Water Purification Plant and Pumping Station was the first of several updated facilities in the century since. Columbus remains on the forefront of wastewater treatment methods for cities, and to think it all started with experiments.

FLYTOWN

How did an entire neighborhood disappear from the city landscape?

Urban sprawl typically means adding neighborhoods to the city map, not removing them. The unfortunate fate of Flytown means that few people know it even existed.

This section of downtown Columbus near Goodale Street was an entry point for immigrants settling into Columbus in the late 1800s. Flytown was their first home in America, which provided a network of resources. Most Flytown residents were poor immigrants who would eventually become naturalized citizens.

Flytown's popularity eventually led to an urgent need for more housing, which spurred quick and cheap development to accommodate the population surge. Homes that seemed to "fly up" overnight gave Flytown its name. The small homes served the predominantly Irish, Italian, and African American immigrants flowing into the neighborhood.

The small residential section of Flytown added an important international flavor to Columbus, but it was eventually wiped out with a city initiative called the Goodale slum clearance project. The first section of Flytown disappeared around 1955 with the construction of the I-71 and I-670 highways. Further neighborhood development of the Thurber Village project in 1967 eliminated the rest.

The only trace left of Flytown exists on a small marker in Goodale Park next to the highway exit. Although kind words on the plaque immortalize some of Columbus's ethnic roots, it does not tell the full story of the rich history that resides in the name.

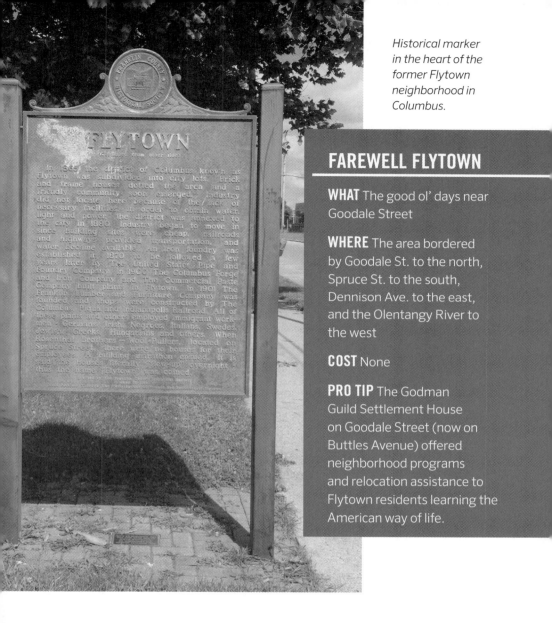

Historical marker in the heart of the former Flytown neighborhood in Columbus.

FAREWELL FLYTOWN

WHAT The good ol' days near Goodale Street

WHERE The area bordered by Goodale St. to the north, Spruce St. to the south, Dennison Ave. to the east, and the Olentangy River to the west

COST None

PRO TIP The Godman Guild Settlement House on Goodale Street (now on Buttles Avenue) offered neighborhood programs and relocation assistance to Flytown residents learning the American way of life.

About seventeen nationalities settled into the Flytown neighborhood, making it one of the most ethnically diverse communities in Columbus.

30

COLUMBUS'S FLAG FLAP

Why it is unusual that the Columbus City flag is on a flagpole at City Hall?

No one can fully appreciate the Columbus City flag that is flying at City Hall, because it is an expected image in the heart of the city. What makes Columbus's official flag unique is that it took sixty-three years to get onto the flagpole due to its confusing history.

The idea for an official municipal flag had its conception in the coat of arms adopted by the Columbus City Council in 1912. However, it wasn't until 1929 that anyone thought about designing a flag from it with a specific design, colors, and symbol.

Once produced, it took several more decades before anyone could see it flying because flags were expensive in the 1950s, so Columbus officials only purchased one. It stayed protected in an envelope in the city clerk's office for another twenty years.

By the 1970s the first city flags began appearing publicly around Columbus. It was an exciting sight until a writer from the National Association of Vexillology stopped into City Hall to photograph some of them in 1974. The flag expert noticed discrepancies in the ones on display.

The coat of arms, per the ordinance, was to be on a blue field with a half wreath of green buckeye leaves and a half circle of sixteen stars. One flag had a coat of arms that was not on a blue background and several other flags

---

By 1974, three different versions of the official Columbus City flag were in use.

Official flag for the City of Columbus.

had buckeye leaves that were brown, not green. Additionally, the colors on the flags were red, white, and blue, not red, white, and yellow, as required by the ordinance.

The Columbus flag controversy was finally put to rest in 1975 when a new and historically correct flag was adopted. Fortunately, the city can now afford enough flags to fly above every city property.

COLUMBUS CITY FLAG

WHAT Controversy surrounding the official symbol of the city for more than half a century

WHERE Any Columbus City building

COST None

PRO TIP The colors on the flag are a combination of the Italian and Spanish flags, arranged in equal-width bands, honoring the Italian roots and Spanish heritage of Christopher Columbus, after whom the city is named.

31

NOSTALGIC DOWNTOWN SANDWICH

What made a downtown lunchtime favorite so famous?

Downtown workers have their favorite lunchtime options, but no fare will ever match the popularity of the Barnes Drug Store Open-Faced Toasted Cheese Sandwich. The Barnes Drug Store and the toasted cheese sandwich are long gone, but the nostalgia has never left the area surrounding 44 East Broad Street.

The Barnes Drug Store was the place to go for lunch downtown in the 1930s, '40s, and '50s. There were few eateries in the area at the time, so it is not surprising that the cheese sandwich developed a cult following. What made it so special? Perhaps it was the addition of cream cheese and mayonnaise or just the perfect taste of comfort food with the right kind of conversation. Whatever the reason, the open-faced toasted cheese sandwich became a staple for three decades in the downtown lunchtime scene.

For a time, it appeared that the memories and secret recipe of the sandwich disappeared with the 1969 demolition of the Outlook Building, which housed the drug store. Fortunately, the son of Paul "Doc" Barnes eventually decided to reveal the family recipe.

The Barnes Drug Store was demolished in 1969 to make way for the James A. Rhodes State Office Tower.

The famous street-front lunch destination at the Barnes Drug Store is now occupied by the Rhodes State Office Tower.

THE BARNES DRUG STORE

WHAT Once served the most famous sandwich in downtown Columbus

WHERE In a lot now occupied by the Rhodes State Office Tower

COST Minimal for the ingredients to make a legendary Columbus lunchtime treat

PRO TIP Adjust the proportions of the sandwich ingredients to accommodate your personal taste.

Though the physical building is gone, a taste of the downtown nostalgia is now possible with the cheese sandwich recipe in print:

The Barnes Drug Store Open-Faced Cheese

Sandwich

1 lb. Philadelphia Cream Cheese

½ lb. shredded cheddar cheese

2 Tbsp. Hellman's Real Mayonnaise

1 Tbsp. dry or prepared mustard

Salt

A slice of bread

Mix cheeses together with a fork. Mix in the mayonnaise. Add the mustard and a pinch of salt and mix all ingredients thoroughly. Let the mixture reach room temperature. Pre-toast one side of a slice of bread in the broiler or oven. Spread the cheese mixture on the untoasted side of bread and place into the broiler or oven. When the cheese is bubbly and starting to brown, it is time to remove it and enjoy.

HISTORICALLY SQUIRRELLY BEHAVIOR

What is behind Columbus's odd obsession with squirrels?

It seems that Columbus has always has a thing for squirrels. The native gray squirrel is a welcome sight in nearly every city park, but Columbus residents have not always been so fond of them. After a series of negative events against the squirrels throughout Columbus's history, it is a wonder that the small rodents ever returned.

Early city settlers considered the gray squirrel a nuisance. In all fairness, the small animals brought the hostile attitude on themselves by routinely destroying farmers' fields and running ops in granaries to eat the stored food.

In an effort to save crops, the Ohio General Assembly waged war on the rambunctious gray squirrel by requiring property owners to hunt them in 1807. Laws required taxpayers to submit a set number of squirrel scalps along with their taxes. Each township set their own limits, which ranged from ten to one hundred scalps. Those who came up short faced fines, whereas those who submitted over the quota received additional pay.

Despite these requirements, the squirrels continued to overrun properties in such extensive numbers that city leaders in Franklin County became concerned about injury to farmers in the fields. The escalating concerns prompted massive organized community hunts.

Female gray squirrels produce ten to twelve offspring per year.

A gray squirrel frolics in Goodale Park in downtown Columbus.

COLUMBUS'S GRAY SQUIRREL

WHAT A target for early settlers and beloved modern-day park companions

WHERE Throughout Columbus parks

COST A lot of squirrel lives in the 1800s

PRO TIP Current laws restrict hunting seasons and bag limits for the gray squirrel.

The first hunt, on April 19–20, 1822, netted nine thousand squirrels. In August of that year the Ohio General Assembly placed an ad in the *Columbus Gazette* calling for all citizens to join another a community hunt. Townships each chose representatives to attend a "hunting caucus" at the home of early settler and civic leader Christian Heyl. Residents took to the fields and streets and even waded in the Scioto River to kill as many squirrels as they could carry. Within several hours, 19,600 squirrel scalps were collected.

33 FAMOUS UNKNOWN BOY SCOUT

Where is there a tribute to an anonymous Boy Scout?

It seems absurd that there could be an effort to bring fame and honor to a Boy Scout, yet no one knows his name. A plaque on the grounds of the Ohio Statehouse commemorates the honorable actions of a young man who remains nameless despite his public recognition.

The plaque, located on a rock on the North Plaza of the Statehouse, reads "Dedicated to the Unknown Boy Scout." It is believed that the young boy helped an American man named William Boyce, who was visiting London and had difficulty navigating the neighborhoods. The boy assisted him through the foggy streets of London, and the man was grateful. Boyce offered to tip the young

UNKNOWN BOY SCOUT PLAQUE

WHAT A public tribute to a commendable Boy Scout whom no one knows

WHERE A rock on North Statehouse Plaza near the corner of Broad and High Sts.

COST None

PRO TIP While searching for the Boy Scout plaque take note of some of the other hidden plaques and features on the north plaza including a bee aviary.

An additional plaque commemorating the seventy-fifth anniversary of the Central Ohio Council of the Boy Scouts of America sits beneath the Unknown Boy Scout Plaque.

The Unknown Boy Scout Plaque on the corner of the Statehouse North Plaza.

man, but he refused the gesture. The boy indicated that he was a Scout and explained that he assisted out of civic duty and nothing more.

Upon his return to the United States, Boyce became an instrumental founder of the Boy Scouts of America. In doing so, he never forgot the kind gesture of that young English boy in London who adhered to the same principles that the Scouts aspire to today. It is believed that the plaque was placed at the Ohio Statehouse during a Boy Scouts of America celebration of their 25th anniversary in 1935.

34 HOUSING MORE THAN MILITARY SUPPLIES

What war secrets live behind the fences at DSCC?

It is easy to feel curious when passing by the sprawling complex of the Defense Supply Center of Columbus on Yearling Road. It is so grand and guarded on every side that passers-by cannot help but wonder, what goes on in there? The name alone provides some insight, but most people in Columbus are unaware of the significance of DSCC to global military operations. Even fewer people know about the war secrets hidden behind the tall fence line of the facility.

DSCC is one of Columbus's largest employers, with more than nine thousand Department of Defense civilians, military personnel, and contractors. The complex is so large that is resembles a small city, complete with a daycare, salon, golf course, swimming pool, park, café, and a twenty-four-hour food market. The complex's fenced-in perimeter provides only a small glimpse of the large buildings and military vehicles inside.

The facility has played an important role in every major military operation since World War I. When the U.S. military needed a new defense supply depot in 1918, Columbus was a prime location because of its proximity to three railroad lines. It was ideal for weapon distribution to other military facilities.

DSCC was originally called the Columbus Quartermaster Reserve Depot and still operates as one of the most significant military installations in the world.

One of several guarded entrances to the Defense Supply Center of Columbus.

DEFENSE SUPPLY CENTER COLUMBUS (DSCC)

WHAT A main supply center for the United States military

WHERE 401 N Yearling Rd.

COST None

PRO TIP Do not attempt to enter the DSCC property unless you are authorized personnel.

During World War II, DSCC emerged as the largest military installation in the world. The facility employed more than ten thousand civilians and maintained warehouses for the highest level of military weapons and supplies. During that time, DSCC also converted some of the warehouses into encampments for more than four hundred German prisoners of war.

The six original warehouses in the DSCC complex were demolished in 2000 to make room for other military needs. Today, DSCC still provides parts and supplies to all branches of the U.S. military around the world.

35

RINGSIDE TREASURE

Where is the oldest bar in Columbus hidden with its treasured sports memorabilia?

It would seem that Columbus's oldest bar might have a big enough reputation that it would be easy to find, but the secluded location of the Ringside Café is part of its charm.

Tucked away in the maze of downtown's Pearl Alley, Ringside's corner façade resembles a place that might require an exclusive invite or secret handshake to enter. Perhaps the cozy tavern did require more classified credentials back when it first opened in 1897. After all, Ringside Café was the hangout for Columbus's social and political elite in its early years.

In keeping with its name, Ringside Café is a treasure trove of boxing memorabilia, including photos, paintings, and an original ringside bell. For the past 100-plus years, all of the items were acquired and passed along as the saloon, tavern, speakeasy, and now restaurant changed hands.

RINGSIDE CAFE

WHAT Columbus's oldest bar

WHERE 19 N Pearl St.

COST Approximately $10 for the 100% Angus chuck "Ali" burger

PRO TIP Because the restaurant is tucked away in a downtown alley, opt for parking at a meter on Gay Street or in a nearby paid lot.

As a speakeasy during the Roaring Twenties, the Ringside Café operated under the name of the Jolly Gargoyle.

Ringside Café is tucked away in the winding Pearl Alley in the heart of downtown Columbus.

The Ringside Café has a rich history of wins and losses, like the famous boxers that it commemorates on the tavern walls. It was originally the Board of Trade Saloon, where local notables made business deals and talked politics. A fire destroyed the tavern in 1909, and it was resurrected as the Chamber of Commerce Café. It had a few good years of serving brew and even becoming a speakeasy during Prohibition.

The private establishment became more mainstream in 1960 when it emerged as Clem's Ringside. Clem's had a long run until 2008 when it sold and the new owners gave it some much-needed updating to what downtown regulars now enjoy as the Ringside Café.

The tiny bar and restaurant serve up some of the best hamburgers in the city, which are named after famous boxers, like the "Ali" and the "Oscar De La Hoya."

36

HIS LIPS ARE SEALED

Why does a famous local monument to Chief Leatherlips have no lips?

It is a fair question given that Chief Leatherlips lived to pursue peace between the Native American Indians and the white man in the late eighteenth and early nineteenth centuries. He was a highly regarded Ohio Wyandot Chief who got his name because he was so trusted. When Chief Leatherlips gave his word, it was as solid as leather.

CHIEF LEATHERLIPS MONUMENT

WHAT A tribute monument to one of the great Wyandot Indian Chiefs in Ohio

WHERE 7377 Riverside Dr. in Scioto Park in Dublin

COST None

PRO TIP Walk to the top of Leatherlips's head for a memorable photo with the entire monument.

The twelve-foot-high monument that pays tribute to the chief, whose Indian name is Shateyahronyah, is made from local limestone and designed in a three-dimensional puzzle-like structure. Commissioned by the Dublin Arts Council, artist Ralph Helmick designed Leatherlips to protrude from the hillside with his hair blowing back in the wind.

While the limestone image of Leatherlips is meticulously detailed, it is hard not to notice that the sculpture has no lips. Perhaps this is because Leatherlips was silenced forever in June 1810. Leatherlips was instrumental in the signing of the Treaty of Greenville with white settlers in 1795, costing Native Americans much of their land in Ohio. This created a divide within the Wyandot tribes and angered Tecumseh, who advocated forcing the enemy away.

Leatherlips was accused of witchcraft and sentenced

The Chief Leatherlips Monument on the hillside in Dublin Park.

to death by a tribunal, led by his own brother, Wyandot Chief Roundhead.

The statue in Scioto Park symbolically overlooks the land that Chief Leatherlips signed over to white settlers.

The Chief Leatherlips Monument was dedicated in Scioto Park in July 1990 and remains a popular picnic spot.

37

A BIG IMPRESSION

Where is there a topiary garden in the form of an impressionist painting?

The topiary park in downtown Columbus is one of the most extravagant and exciting public displays in the city, but many Columbus natives have never seen it. If you love gardens, you won't want to miss this horticultural masterpiece.

Tucked behind the Columbus Metropolitan Library and the old Ohio School for the Deaf is a life-size topiary rendition of George Seurat's impressionist painting *A Sunday Afternoon on the Island of La Grande Jatte*. The public park is a secluded treasure where visitors can sit

Life size topiaries of impressionist painting A Sunday Afternoon on the Isle of La Grande Jatte *fill the lawn at the Topiary Park in Columbus.*

among the fifty-four life-size topiary figures on the grounds for a picnic lunch or a quiet moment on a bench. In addition to the life-size topiary replicas of the people in the painting, the boats on the water and animals are also created as topiary sculptures.

The development of the topiary park was instrumental in reviving the neighborhood in the late 1980s. Once the Ohio School for the Deaf moved operations in 1953, the neighborhood

---

The tallest sculpture in the topiary park is twelve feet high.

Close-up of life-size topiary statues depicting a famous impressionist painting behind the Old Deaf School Park.

TOPIARY PARK

WHAT A living topiary representation of a famous impressionist painting

WHERE 480 E Town St., behind the Columbus Metropolitan Library

COST None

PRO TIP Stop by the gatehouse, which is also a gift shop for unique gifts and more information about the garden.

declined. A fire in 1981 destroyed most of the buildings that were left on the school's ten acres of land. A year later, the district, left with little pride, was designated as a historic district, opening the door for a new vision.

The topiary park is the phoenix of community pride that rose from the ashes of urban blight. Business and neighborhood association donations made it possible for local artist James T. Mason to construct the first wire frames and plant shrubs in 1988.

The topiary park is Columbus's finest example of living art that is as beautiful covered in snow in the winter as it is in full bloom in the summer.

What happened to the Statehouse dome that was designed to be there?

At first glance, it is easy to miss that the Ohio Statehouse in downtown Columbus does not actually have the dome that is typical of most statehouses. In fact, Ohio is one of only eleven statehouses without a signature dome. The structure on top of the building is a cupola, but that was not in the original design.

So why did the capitol building dome in the original architectural design disappear?

The answer starts with an 1838 nationwide contest to design the Ohio Statehouse. The Statehouse Act commissioned a three-member panel to judge sixty entries. The top three submissions were similar in design, but each featured appealing differences. When the panel could not commit to a single design, they opted to combine the best features of each. An architectural consultant named Alexander Jackson Davis created the merged design but opted for a cupola instead of a dome.

Despite the agreed-upon blueprint, the design went through several renditions over the years, with a dome option on and off several times. The time lapse between the beginning of construction in 1839 and end of construction in 1861 resulted in a lack of consistency in who executed the blueprint and which version they had in hand.

In the end, the decision came down to Isaiah Rogers, a Cincinnati architect who oversaw the final stages of

The Ohio Statehouse cupola is sixty-four feet across and seventy feet tall.

The Ohio Statehouse cupola is often mistaken for a traditional statehouse dome.

construction. He sided with the cupola design for the roof of the Greek Revival-style statehouse.

Though the cupola slightly resembles a dome, is differs in that the two-story structure is flat on top versus the traditional dome shape. Many visitors to the Ohio Statehouse do not pay much attention to the alternative top even though the cupola is its most striking feature.

THE OHIO STATEHOUSE CUPOLA

WHAT The Statehouse features a cupola instead of a typical capitol building dome.

WHERE Downtown Columbus on Capitol Square

COST None

PRO TIP Take one of the free tours of the Statehouse to walk the spiral staircase and experience the thirty-one-foot- wide skylight in the cupola.

39

A DISPLAY OF CHAMPIONS

Where did Columbus host the world's largest Wheaties display?

It is no secret that Columbus is a thriving test market for brands that are launching new products, especially in the food industry. So when General Mills wanted to showcase

Riverwatch Tower occupies the land that garnered world-wide attention in the early twentieth century.

its Wheaties breakfast cereal in 1938, the company turned to Columbus for a larger-than-life and memorable marketing campaign. Wheaties was the company's first ready-to-eat cereal, eventually becoming known as the "breakfast of champions."

The original Big Bear grocery store on West Lane Avenue, now the Riverwatch Tower apartments, was home to the World's Largest

Wheaties display. The elaborate display showcased more than 46,550,000 Wheaties flakes in the store. The display was a grand-scale publicity stunt that would never be able to

Wheaties cereal cost ten cents a box in 1938 during the General Mills promotion.

The world's largest Wheaties display in Big Bear grocery in 1938. Credit: Ohio History Connection.

WORLD'S LARGEST WHEATIES DISPLAY

WHAT General Mills' 1938 Wheaties promotion in Columbus

WHERE The location is now home to the Riverwatch Tower Apartment at 386 W Lane Ave.

COST Nostalgia

PRO TIP Though the display and Big Bear store are gone, you can impress your friends with trivia as you pass by the current Riverwatch Tower location.

happen today because it took up too much precious aisle space.

The Wheaties promotion garnered so much attention that General Mills decided to make it even bigger by tying in Columbus's love of baseball. The company guaranteed a case of Wheaties to any baseball player who hit a home run. That worked out well for local player Nick Cullop, who happened to be proficient at homers. Cullop racked up so many home-run Wheaties wins that he had to rent a truck to haul his load.

True to the philanthropic form of many Columbusites, Cullop donated all of his boxes of Wheaties to charity.

40

NATIONAL ROAD NOSTALGIA

Are there any National Road mile markers left in Columbus?

Drivers on East Main Street or West Broad Street on the fringes of Columbus may notice occasional abandoned stones with unique markings. These are important remnants of the old National Road, now U.S. Route 40, that passes through the city. There are only a few left to observe, but the discovery is enlightening, especially with an understanding their significance.

The Ohio National Road is part of a 700-mile stretch of roadway that runs from Maryland to St. Louis, jogging through Pennsylvania, West Virginia, Ohio, Indiana, and Illinois. At one point, more than 600 mile markers followed the length of the road. Most of them have disappeared.

The markers more closely resemble headstones and are often mistaken for such, but close examination reveals an important part of Columbus and U.S. history. Each oddly shaped marker stands three feet high and is chiseled with the word "Cumberland" (for Cumberland, Maryland, where the road began) and the names and distances of the next-closest towns.

The National Road reached Columbus in 1833. Congress stipulated that the National Road had to pass through

The Historic National Road through Ohio was designated as an All-American Road National Scenic Byway in 2002 by the Federal Highway Administration.

One of the only remaining National Road mile markers in Columbus, located on Broad Street in downtown Columbus.

NATIONAL ROAD MILE MARKERS

WHAT Remnants of historical mile markers along the National Road through Columbus

WHERE E Main St. to W Broad St.

COST None

PRO TIP National Road mile markers were only placed on the north sides of the roads, so if you set out to look for them, this will help narrow the search.

capital cities maintaining as straight of a course as possible and be marked at regular intervals. However, the road through Columbus is anything but straight. Local merchants protested and managed to detour the road instead of keeping it on Main Street through downtown. It zig-zags through the city, entering Columbus on Main Street from the east and exiting on Broad Street to the west.

The few National Road markers left are difficult to find. One of the easiest to see is located in downtown Columbus on Broad Street between the Scioto River bridge and the new Veteran's Memorial.

There are several other mile markers scattered in the city near the east side of Columbus along East Main Street near Reynoldsburg and also in Bexley.

41

SWINE-INSPIRED LANDFILLS

What is the connection between Columbus landfills and local pigs?

It is difficult to give much attention to Columbus's main landfill unless the wind is blowing in just right direction, forcing commuters to look as they pass by the Grove City

Current cells being filled with trash delivered from two transfer stations in Columbus.

facility. Trash collection is something that seems to have always been a part of life in the city, and it is easily taken for granted.

While the modern-day Franklin County Sanitary Landfill, operated by the Solid Waste Authority of Central Ohio (SWACO), is a highly engineered facility, residents owe thanks to life as we know it to local swine in the 1940s.

During a population boom in Columbus in the early twentieth century, the city faced new challenges with garbage disposal. Incinerators could not keep up with the refuse coming from the metropolitan area. The solution was to follow a nationwide trend and ship the extra garbage off to local pig farms.

Each person in Columbus generates four to five pounds of waste per day, resulting in 4,200 tons of trash going to the landfill daily.

The view of the Franklin County Sanitary Landfill from the roadway.

Inset: Franklin County Sanitary Landfill entrance on London-Groveport Road.

FRANKLIN COUNTY SANITARY LANDFILL

WHAT Diseased swine inspired Columbus's current method of waste disposal

WHERE 3851 London-Groveport Rd. in Grove City

COST None

PRO TIP For the truly intrigued, the Solid Waste Authority of Central Ohio (SWACO) offers free public tours of the Franklin County Sanitary Landfill several times per year.

That system worked well until the U.S. Public Health Service noticed an increase in trichinosis in swine eating the untreated garbage. Franklin County officials needed a new system, but the options were slim in 1951. They decided to sell bonds and build three holes in the ground, called landfills, unknowingly altering the procedures for garbage disposal forever.

The landfill concept evolved over the decades. In 1988, House Bill 592 changed the discourse over trash disposal, making it a more environmentally friendly mission. The Franklin County Sanitary Landfill is highly engineered to maximize landfill space and use technology to plan for decades to come. Part of the modern-day waste disposal strategy is to reduce the amount of refuse to begin with by encouraging recycling.

Technology and disposal techniques at the landfill also make it possible to stand in the center of the dump site and not see trash or smell it. Odor neutralizers border the facility.

42

SCANDAL TIPS THE SCALES OF JUSTICE

Where is a scandalous judge still showcased in Columbus?

The elements involved in one of Columbus's most epic public scandals have all the makings of a movie plot: a prominent judge, his dying wife, a mistress, and lots of expensive jewels. Although Judge Homer Bostwick never made it to the big screen, his photo still graces the hallways of the Franklin County Probate Court as one of the most prominent judges in Columbus. Hundreds of people walk by his photo every day unaware of the saga behind it.

Judge Homer Bostwick was a revered voice in the Franklin County courts during his term from 1917 to 1931. His one-month relationship with a mistress named Opal Eversole, from May to June of 1931, was his judicial undoing. Judge Bostwick bestowed many gifts upon Opal during their brief time together, including

JUDGE HOMER BOSTWICK

WHAT A photo of Judge Homer Bostwick still hangs on the walls of the Franklin County Probate Court.

WHERE 373 S High St., 22nd Floor

COST None

PRO TIP The Judge Bostwick story appeared in a *TIME Magazine* article titled "The Indian-Giving Judge" and remains one of the most notable scandals in Franklin County history.

Fallout from the Judge Bostwick scandal resulted in strict morality conduct rules for probate judges that are still in effect today.

The photo of Homer Bostwick still hangs on the wall among prominent probate judges at the Franklin County Courthouse.

an expensive Auburn automobile and jewelry belonging to his dying wife, Estella. In the jewelry stash was Estella's diamond ring, which he deemed safe to dispose of since Estella was on her deathbed.

Unfortunately for Judge Bostwick, Estella made a miraculous and unexpected recovery. Had things gone as planned, the relationship might have remained unnoticed. Instead, the fallout became a public soap opera and courthouse embarrassment.

Things got sticky when Judge Bostwick attempted to recover the ring. Opal claimed the jewelry as hers. The scandal exploded when Opal was taken to jail after causing a scene at the courthouse and was eventually forced to give up the ring.

Judge Bostwick was removed from the bench with a tarnished reputation and a dismal end to an otherwise respectable career as a judge. After seven court cases related to his dismissal, Judge Bostwick was disbarred for immorality and misconduct in office.

43 RAILROAD CAR SANCTUARY

Where do famous retired train cars find new purpose?

Tucked away at the end of Old Henderson Road in northwest Columbus on a plot of land surrounded by a few businesses and residential neighborhoods is a train lover's playground.

THE DEPOT RAIL MUSEUM

WHAT A stunning preservation of railroad history hidden in northwest Columbus

WHERE 921 Old Henderson Rd.

COST None unless you book an event

PRO TIP You can rent the Ringling Bros. executive car for your next business meeting and absorb the karma of the success from the deals that took place in that exact parlor car.

It is the kind of place so hidden that no one would ever accidentally find it. That is what makes The Depot such a treasure in Columbus.

The Depot Rail Museum is an 1880s train depot that was relocated on this plot of land in 2003. Sitting on the grounds are some of the most unique and storied train cars in railroad history. Some of the more notable cars include the executive parlor car for the Ringling Bros. Circus, called Car 100, and the Vulcan Locomotive, which was the limestone-hauling workhorse

The Ringling Bros. executive Car 100 was the backdrop for legendary deals between businessmen like Diamond Jim Brady and John Skelton Williams during the Gilded Age.

Top left: The hidden Depot Rail Museum in north Columbus. Credit: Barry Fromm.

Top right: The caboose at The Depot Rail Museum is one of several train cars on the property. Credit: Barry Fromm.

Bottom left: Parlor area from inside Car 100 at The Depot Rail Museum. Credit: Barry Fromm.

Bottom right: Living quarters inside the caboose at The Depot Rail Museum. Credit: Barry Fromm.

for the New York Central Railroad. One of the prized cars on the property is a wooden caboose built in Vermont in 1909.

The Depot features rare furniture and antiques that once graced train cars as well as a one-third scale Scioto Valley Railroad Train. A dining car from the Great Northern Railway is rented out for events, and the interior of The Depot is transformed to accommodate small conferences and meetings.

While The Depot rents train cars and space for private events, they have tours for small groups and occasionally hold public programs throughout the year.

SMELLY SUCCESS

Where is Columbus hiding a plant that is world-famous for its stench?

Chances are as remote as winning the lottery that Columbusites will smell their way to the hidden corpse flower, as it is rarely in bloom, but seeing it even in its non-blooming state is a unique treat. The Ohio State University Biological Sciences Greenhouse is home to several species of the titan arum, more commonly known as the corpse flower.

When the plant produces one of its rare blooms, which can happen at any time without warning and sometimes a decade apart, it is a worldwide spectacle. The blooms are six to eight feet tall with an unmistakable scent that resembles a rotting corpse, which is how it derived its nickname. The large plant grows naturally in rainforests. It is a considered an unbranched inflorescence, which is a floral plant made up of smaller flowers. Even out of bloom the plant can produce leaves that reach up to 20 feet high.

Once a plant blooms, it is customary for conservatories to name them. The successful titan arum collection at OSU includes the names of notable Ohio Buckeyes like "Woody," for OSU coaching legend Woody Hayes; "Maudine," a famous campus cow that was also crowned OSU's Homecoming Queen in 1926; and "Jesse," in honor of OSU alum and Olympian track star Jesse Owens.

OSU biologists have successfully celebrated five titan arum blooms since 2011. The first bloom happened ten years after its seeds were planted. Though the prized collection of rare plants at the OSU Biological Sciences Greenhouse seems like a well-kept secret, the greenhouse has regular visiting hours during the week.

"Woody" was the first titan arum to bloom in the OSU Biological Sciences collection. Credit: The Ohio State University.

Inset: A little girl holds her nose at the smell of the corpse flower in bloom. Credit: The Ohio State University.

A mature corpse flower showcases its rare and famous blooms once every two to ten years, and it only lasts for a few hours.

CORPSE FLOWER COLLECTION

WHAT Several species of the titan arum growing in Columbus can bloom at any time.

WHERE OSU Biological Sciences Greenhouse, 332 W 12th Ave.

COST None

PRO TIP Sign up for bloom alerts for the titan arum "Woody" plant on its dedicated Facebook page.

<u>45</u> CUTTING-EDGE COMMUNITY

What area of Columbus was the prototype for insulated communities?

Most communities throughout Columbus, and nationwide, are sectioned to include modern conveniences like grocery stores, banks, post offices, and retail shops in proximity. This is how modern-day residents identify with neighborhoods. But the concept of a self-sufficient neighborhood was not always a way of life until a 1.4-square-mile residential pocket of Columbus called Forest Park decided to test the idea in 1961.

The Forest Park of today is a section of northeast Columbus that more or less serves as a pass-through to someplace else. Most Columbus natives know this area for the nearby former Northland Mall, which was Columbus's first shopping mall in 1964, but tiny Forest Park was also the first residential community located in the city.

The idea of a self-sufficient community started in Forest Park, with the concept of combining shopping and recreation into one place that was easily accessible to the neighborhood. They built shopping centers, a bowling alley, restaurants, childcare centers, convenience stores, storage facilities, and swimming pools.

Forest Park derived its name from the abundance of trees in the area that line most streets and adorn nearly all residential properties.

One of several entrances onto Tamarack Circle in the Forest Park community.

Inset: Welcome sign to the Forest Park community.

FOREST PARK NEIGHBORHOOD

WHAT The first residential community in Columbus and where the concept of a self-sufficient neighborhood started

WHERE Tamarack Circle

COST None

PRO TIP Northland Mall, the retail crown jewel of Forest Park for 38 years, is now the location of a government complex located near Karl Road and S.R. 161.

The Tamarack Circle roundabout served as the hub that connected all of the community conveniences. The central location still services residents along the Morse Road, Karl Road, and State Route 161 corridors. The one-mile roundabout encompasses restaurants, shops, a grocery, a beverage drive-thru, an ice cream parlor, a church, and other conveniences.

Forest Park West, west of Karl Road, came first in the 1960s, followed by the development of Forest Park East that started in 1965. This was the first time that a community tried this kind of cohesive way of living, which is now common in neighborhoods nationwide.

A DISTRICT FIT FOR A KING

How did the king of the Brewery District fall into the role?

The jolly King Gambrinus statue on Front Street downtown seems to be an appropriate symbol for welcoming visitors to Columbus's thriving Brewery District. The odd, large, clunky, and colorful statue is the mythological king of beer said to have special brewing powers. Perhaps that is why Gambrinus was the most popular brand of beer for August Wagner Breweries, which originally showcased the statue in the early 1900s.

August Wagner Breweries operated in Columbus from 1906 to 1919. It remained through 1974, changing hands many times over the decades. The King stood the test of time, keeping watch over the beer flowing out of the plant. When the brewery closed and the building was demolished, everything, including the statue of the King, was hauled to the trash pile.

When the Dispatch Printing Company purchased the land in 1975, they also purchased the King and restored the statue to its former elegance. With no brewery to guard, the King was placed in a park at Front and Sycamore Streets. For twenty-five years, the King guarded a

KING GAMBRINUS STATUE

WHAT The mascot of a defunct brewery that found an appropriate home in Columbus's Brewery District

WHERE Front St. between Sycamore and Beck Sts.

COST None

PRO TIP While you are in the neighborhood, stop in one of the many craft breweries in the district and raise a glass to the King.

King Gambrinus serving as a centerpiece in Columbus's Brewery District.

vacant lot with his celebratory disposition stomping his foot on a keg and wearing a crown on his head just as he did when he first appeared in Columbus.

When the Brewery District started to flourish in the 2000s, the King was moved to a new throne. He is the street-level guard for the Brewery District on Front Street, which could not be more fitting for the district that celebrates everything beer. It was a long road, but it appears that King Gambrinus is now guarding the kingdom he was meant to protect.

The statue of King Gambrinus, the mythological king of beer that rules the Brewery District, is more than a century old.

COVER THAT UP

Is there such a thing as decent public exposure?

It is hard to imagine in the current politically correct state of society that there would ever be a law specifically targeting diseased, disfigured, or unattractive people. But things were indeed different in 1959. That is when the City of Columbus passed an ordinance making it illegal for unsightly people to expose themselves in public.

INDECENT EXPOSURE LAW

WHAT The odd city ordinance that outlaws unsightly people from exposing themselves is still in effect.

WHERE Throughout Columbus

COST None, unless you are arrested

PRO TIP Do not tempt fate by testing the archaic ordinance as laws have broadened and are enforced.

Ordinance 2387.04, titled "Exposing self when unsightly," falls under a broader category of "Vagrants and Suspicious Persons." Besides the mentions that one might expect prohibiting loitering and possession of narcotics, there is a small provision at the very end targeting the less-than-appealing who are deemed a public nuisance.

The ordinance reads: "No person, being in any way diseased, maimed, mutilated or deformed so as to be an unsightly or disgusting object, shall expose himself to public view upon any street, sidewalk or in any park or other public place for the purpose of soliciting alms or exciting sympathy, interest or curiosity."

Though the law still stands, it is not enforced by 1959 standards. Instead, it is more broadly enforced by Columbus Police as public indecency and includes several categories of offenses.

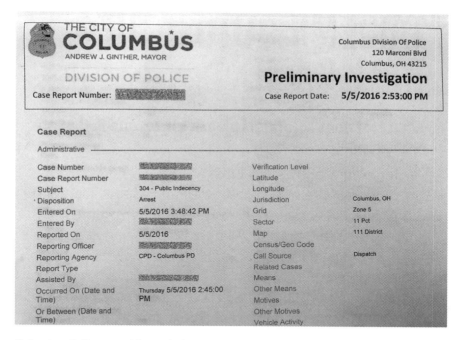

THE CITY OF
COLUMBUS
ANDREW J. GINTHER, MAYOR

DIVISION OF POLICE

Columbus Division Of Police
120 Marconi Blvd
Columbus, OH 43215

Preliminary Investigation

Case Report Number:

Case Report Date: **5/5/2016 2:53:00 PM**

Case Report

Administrative

Case Number		Verification Level	
Case Report Number		Latitude	
Subject	304 - Public Indecency	Longitude	
Disposition	Arrest	Jurisdiction	Columbus, OH
Entered On	5/5/2016 3:48:42 PM	Grid	Zone 5
Entered By		Sector	11 Pct
Reported On	5/5/2016	Map	111 District
Reporting Officer		Census/Geo Code	
Reporting Agency	CPD - Columbus PD	Call Source	Dispatch
Report Type		Related Cases	
Assisted By		Means	
Occurred On (Date and Time)	Thursday 5/5/2016 2:45:00 PM	Other Means	
Or Between (Date and Time)		Motives	
		Other Motives	
		Vehicle Activity	

Columbus Police report for an indecent exposure arrest.

The City of Columbus's vagrant and suspicious persons ordinance of 1959 also prohibits the inhalation of nail polish.

48 TAKE ME OUT TO THE BALL GAME

What role does Columbus play in big league ball game traditions?

An aerial view above 1155 West Mound Street still shows the outline of the old Cooper Stadium baseball diamond. It is where many memories were made as residents cheered on the Columbus Clippers minor league baseball team, ringing cowbells during home runs and filling up on dime-a-dog night.

The Columbus Clippers' new home is Huntington Park in the downtown Arena District. The team and the park draw large crowds on summer nights, but their original home, which many Columbusites remember, is the site of many baseball firsts.

Originally called Red Bird Stadium, the Mound Street field was the first ballpark in the country built with stadium lights, making night games possible and the spectacle of post-game fireworks a part of ballgame tradition.

HUNTINGTON PARK

WHAT Baseball stadium of the Columbus Clippers

WHERE Downtown in the heart of the Arena District

COST Lawn tickets start at $5

PRO TIP Nearly every Clippers game has a promotion for discounted tickets or food.

The term "southpaw," used for left-handed pitchers, came from Columbus baseball when a reporter used the nickname to describe player Eddie "Cannonball" Morris.

Columbus Clippers baseball game at Huntington Park in Columbus. Credit: Columbus Clippers.

Inset: Remnants of Cooper Stadium still appear as a faint version of this 1981 aerial view. Credit: Columbus Metropolitan Library.

Columbus baseball at the old Cooper Stadium is where hungry fans first heard the echoes of "Get 'em while they're hot," the famous crowd call of vendors selling sausages. The stadium is also where Franklin Delano Roosevelt made the opening speech of his first presidential campaign.

Predating Cooper Stadium and the Columbus Clippers was Neil Park, Columbus's first concrete stadium, and the Columbus Senators team. It was here that Columbus likely made its greatest contribution to the game of baseball, with the tradition of playing "The Star-Spangled Banner" before a game.

During the opening day game at Neil Park the governor gave a speech, and the band excited the crowd of fifteen thousand fans with patriotic music, culminating with "The Star-Spangled Banner." The exuberant crowd stood on their feet, singing along, and that is when a national baseball tradition was born.

Now you can experience these baseball traditions that started in Columbus at the Columbus Clippers home games at Huntington Park.

49

MORE THAN MIRACLES INSIDE THE GROTTO

What treasures reside in the roadside Grotto with the Virgin Mary?

The Grotto that stands proudly in front of the Immaculate Conception Church in Clintonville is a charming public display that showcases the Virgin Mary statue for passing traffic. East North Broadway is a busy east-west thoroughfare through north Columbus. It is unlikely that the commuters who pass the grotto have any idea of the precious stones that reside inside the cave-like structure alongside the Blessed Mother.

One of the few standing grottoes in Columbus, the Immaculate Conception Church structure was erected in 1961 as a dedication to the Virgin Mary. The grotto was constructed with stones collected around the world by parishioners. The intricate details inside are assemblies of marble, granite, obsidian, rose quartz, iron ore, limestone, and coal. The stones came from every state in the union and from many countries, including Israel.

IMMACULATE CONCEPTION CHURCH & GROTTO

WHAT One of the most unique grottoes in the world, constructed with storied stones that surround the Virgin Mary statue

WHERE 414 E North Broadway in Clintonville

COST None

PRO TIP The grotto faces south, so the best times to view the intricate stones in the concave structure is in the early morning or late afternoon.

The grotto at the Immaculate Conception Church in Clintonville offers treasures behind the Virgin Mary statue.

The Virgin Mary statue is the centerpiece at the Immaculate Conception Church, unlike other grottoes around the world that typically place the statue in a cutout on the side.

Like any good biblical reference, the individual stones come with stories and legends, giving them special meaning to the parishioners who collected them. One stone, tucked among the rest is shaped like a Bible. A parishioner named Mary Trenor made that contribution to the construction. Others were hand-collected from places of Christian or ancestral significance.

The unique grotto was designed by an Ohio State University architect named Paul Morill. Only those who take a moment to stop, instead of driving by, will experience the rare treasures that await inside.

50

PIECES OF THE OLD OHIO PEN

Cell doors from the Ohio Pen are used as decorative ivy trellises on the Ohio Moline Plow Building.

Where are there resurrected relics of the old Ohio State Penitentiary?

Columbus's booming downtown Arena District is a $1 billion development that sits on part of the site of the old Ohio Penitentiary that closed in 1984. The thriving district is one of the top destinations in Columbus that includes the Nationwide Arena entertainment venue, Huntington Park baseball field, North Bank Park, restaurants, offices, and condominiums. Artfully disguised among the modern designs in the Arena District are relics of prison cell doors, steel beams, and limestone from the penitentiary fortress.

For nearly a decade, historians fought the demolition of the Ohio Penitentiary, wanting to preserve it and the surrounding twenty-two acres for historical purposes. In the end, the City of Columbus purchased the land, along with fifty acres of neighboring abandoned warehouses and factories, to launch a new vision for the future of downtown Columbus.

Adding to the vibrant energy in the Arena District, relics of an oftentimes dark history pay homage to the Old Pen that

---

When the Ohio Penitentiary closed its doors, it was the oldest maximum security prison in the country operating in an inner city.

The old Ohio Penitentiary before it was demolished. Credit: Columbus Metropolitan Library.

Inset: Wall across from McFerson Commons Park with original Ohio Penitentiary limestone blocks below informational markers.

OHIO PENITENTIARY RELICS

WHAT Historic prison cell doors, steel beams, and limestone from the old Ohio Penitentiary discreetly decorate the popular downtown Arena District.

WHERE Throughout the Arena District

COST None

PRO TIP To identify the original limestone, look for sections that appear more weathered than the rest.

used to occupy the landscape. Look closely at many of the vintage details to find old, repurposed fixtures mixed with the new.

The two flower-and-ivy trellises on the side of the Ohio Moline Plow Building are prison cell doors from the Ohio Penitentiary. Recycled limestone from the prison is found in the retaining walls in North Bank Park and as part of the decorative décor on the Arena Grand Theatre and Burnham Square caretaker's house.

51

SEGREGATED SOCIALIZING

Where are the crumbling remnants of a segregated social scene?

Friendship Park in Gahanna is known for its family-friendly atmosphere and summer music concerts on the lawn. Tucked away in the middle of a residential neighborhood, the park is a hidden gem. Decades before it was a beloved Gahanna park, the twenty acres of land was home to the Big Walnut Country Club, a retreat for prominent African Americans in Columbus in the 1920s. While the country club and much of the information about its history are gone, there are hidden remnants of the elegant segregated social scene literally buried on the grounds. Some of it is still partially visible.

The Big Walnut Country Club opened in 1927 as one of the first African American country clubs in the United States. The most notable names in Columbus African American society gathered at the club to socialize and make business deals. Families held grand picnics in the park on Sundays, and it was the only location where African American newlyweds could hold a reception for friends and relatives in segregated Columbus in the 1950s.

Before the Big Walnut Country Club closed for unknown reasons in the 1950s, it featured a grand clubhouse, golf

BIG WALNUT COUNTRY CLUB

WHAT Remnants of one of the first African American country clubs in the United States

WHERE Friendship Park in Gahanna over the wooden fence on the slope to Big Walnut Creek

COST None

PRO TIP It is safest to view the iron stairs from the top of the slope. Take the precaution of wearing boots if you attempt to go down the hill to view the buried stairs from below, as it is quite steep.

Friendship Park, tucked away in a residential Gahanna neighborhood.

Inset: Stairs leading to Big Walnut Creek from where cottages used to stand at the Big Walnut Country Club.

course, driving range, baseball fields, and cottages.

Although there is no longer any trace of the club in the park, there are two partially buried remnants that still exist. Both are located near the back and right side of the playground on a slope of land leading to Big Walnut Creek.

Just over the wooden fence are pieces of the clubhouse's iron staircase that are visible in the mud on the riverbank. Also visible along the back edge of the park are concrete steps that at one time led from a club cottage to the creek.

The Big Walnut Country Club, a social scene for prominent African Americans, employed mostly white workers from the surrounding neighborhood, which was a rare dynamic in segregated America at the time.

52

COLUMBUS'S FIRST ZOO

Where did Columbus cut its teeth on quality zoo operations in the city?

More than a century before the Columbus Zoo & Aquarium obtained its reputation as one of the top zoos in the country, Columbus featured another zoo that wowed residents with animals from around the world. The short-lived zoo in the Beechwold neighborhood officially lasted as a public zoo for only five months in 1905, but the remnants of its existence are still a delightful sight.

Stone pillars still stand at the entrance of the Beechwold neighborhood.

A drive through the secluded Beechwold neighborhood near Clintonville makes it easy to imagine the zoo grounds that used to be there. The stone entrance leads to a narrow drive surrounded by woods and a tiny roadway barely bigger than the width of a car. The former pedestrian walkway splits in two directions almost immediately as most zoo entrances do. A bridge that reconnects the two walkways farther into the neighborhood is made of the original arched stone. It was known as the "kissing bridge" during the zoo's operations.

Theodore Roosevelt donated several animals to the short-lived Columbus Zoo in the Beechwold neighborhood.

Rustic Bridge is the original stone bridge that connected sections of the zoo.

Inset: Road into the Beechwold neighborhood that used to be pedestrian paths through Columbus's first zoo.

THE FIRST COLUMBUS ZOO

WHAT The first officially named Columbus Zoo that was open to the public for only five months

WHERE The Beechwold neighborhood near Clintonville

COST None

PRO TIP Some of the zoo remnants are located on private property but there are other vestiges to see while walking the neighborhood.

In 1885 some local businessmen invested in the creation of the Columbus Zoological Company. This nineteenth-century version of a start-up business purchased a few hundred acres of land in the Beechwold neighborhood, constructed buildings, and accepted donations of animals. By the fall of 1902, the Columbus Zoological Company had acquired a lion, bears, a rattlesnake, birds, wolves, and a deer.

The zoo opened to the public on May 28, 1905, and filed for bankruptcy by October of that same year. The zoo was dubbed the "Columbus Zoo" by the *Columbus Citizen* newspaper even though competition was brewing nearby from another zoo at Olentangy Park.

Although many of the telltale signs that the area was once a zoo are still visible, others are not so obvious—like a monkey house that is now a converted barn at 150 W. Beechwold Road, located on private property.

HABEEBA'S DANCE OF THE ARTS (page 180)

GRASS SKIRT TIKI ROOM (page 38)

THE CANDY BUCKEYE (page 48)

AUGUST WAGNER BREWERIES (page 92)

CONCRETE CORN (page 138)

COLUMBUS PARK OF ROSES (page 130)

BRISCO ROASTERY AND COFFEE BAR (page 168)

COLUMBUS CULTURAL ARTS CENTER (page 160)

HIGHBANKS METRO PARK LISTENING CHAIR (page 182)

THE PEANUT SHOPPE (page 32)

HUNTINGTON PARK (page 96)

CIRCUS HOUSE SECRETS (page 6)

ROAD TO NOWHERE (page 154)

OHIO JUDICIAL CENTER (page 46)

AIR RAID SHELTER (page 192)

DANCING RABBITS OF BALLANTRAE PARK

What is so significant about the dancing rabbits in a Dublin suburb?

The giant dancing rabbit sculptures in Ballantrae Park in Dublin are eye-catching.

But look closely because these oversized whimsical rabbits gleefully dancing on the hillside are hiding treasures in the metal that are not noticeable without close examination.

Household objects like scissors are imbedded into the sculpture.

Hidden in the details that make up the massive sculptures are scrap metal pieces artistically embedded in the bronze rabbits. Only a close-up look reveals the intricate details that add depth and intrigue to the elegant trio. The items embedded in the metal range from household tools to miniature toys, including a bicycle pedal, scissors, paint gun, chains, looney tunes medallion, coins, sprockets, frying pan, paintbrush, pliers, camera, glove, a rose-pruning tool, and a chip-clip.

The fifteen-foot sculpture, created by English artist Sophie Ryder, mimics the "boxing"

The giant dancing rabbits are three separate sculptures that were installed one by one to create a single masterpiece.

The Dancing Rabbits sculpture at Ballantrae Park in Dublin.

Inset: An up-close look reveals whimsical items like toys and gears in the rabbit sculptures.

THE GIANT DANCING RABBITS OF BALLANTRAE PARK

WHAT A large sculpture of dancing rabbits with household items embedded into the metal

WHERE 6350 Woerner Temple Rd., Dublin, Ohio

COST None

PRO TIP Pack a picnic lunch and enjoy the grounds at Ballantrae Park that surround the dancing rabbits.

hares. It is a mating behavior exhibited during springtime when rabbits appear to box each other for mates. The artist was inspired by the springtime ritual that she witnessed in the Gloucestershire countryside in England where she lives. Ryder wanted to add a hint of adventure to the Dublin sculpture by adding small surprises that require careful attention and observation. The intent is to encourage children to look beyond the obvious and find as many artifacts as possible. The exercise is just as much fun for adults.

The notable sculpture in Dublin was commissioned by Peter Edwards, the developer of the Ballantrae community.

54

GLASS MYTH

How could a myth about one of Columbus's most popular destinations last so long?

The glass atrium over the John F. Wolfe Palm House at the Franklin Park Conservatory is one of the most recognized Columbus landmarks. The Palm House is a sought-after wedding destination featuring more than forty-five species of palms from around the world and a magnificent glass ceiling.

For many years a mystery surrounded how the massive glass atrium even got to Columbus. Even some Columbus history books document that the Palm House atrium was originally featured at the 1893 Chicago World's Fair Columbian Exposition. Historians theorized that the atrium was moved to Columbus because of the 1895 date listed on the Palm House cornerstone. Due to the size and delicate nature of the massive glass piece, no one could properly document how it actually got there.

FRANKLIN PARK CONSERVATORY

WHAT The origins of one of the most recognizable symbols of the Columbus landscape made for an intriguing mystery.

WHERE 1777 E Broad St., Columbus, OH

COST $14 General Admission

PRO TIP Look for the fiddle-leaf fig tree in the Palm House. It is more than 122 years old.

For a period of time between 1927 and 1929, the Palm House housed animals in the lower rooms. These animals eventually became some of the first inhabitants at the Columbus Zoo.

Grand glass atrium of the John F. Wolfe Palm House was designed after a featured structure at the 1893 Chicago World's Fair. Credit: Franklin Park Conservatory and Botanical Gardens.

Inset: Inside the John F. Wolfe Palm House at the Franklin Park Conservatory. Credit: Franklin Park Conservatory and Botanical Gardens.

Upon researching this book, I learned that the reason there is no documentation on the Palm House glass transport is because the story is all a myth. The John F. Wolfe Palm House is only modeled after the great glass house at the Chicago World's Fair, but it is not the original.

The Columbian Exposition at the Chicago World's Fair was a 400th anniversary celebration of Christopher Columbus's arrival in the New World. That event and the elegant structure inspired city officials to duplicate it for a significant horticulture building in the city of Columbus. The John F. Wolfe Palm House opened to the public in 1895 and only coincidentally fell in line with dates that made it appear possible that it was the original structure from Chicago. The myth has lasted almost as long as the structure has been standing.

The massive glass house at the Franklin Park Conservatory protects hundreds of tropical flora and fauna. It is perhaps the most striking feature of the conservatory, welcoming thousands of visitors every year.

55

COLUMBUS'S ROYAL WEDDING

Where is there a tree connected to Columbus's only known royal wedding?

Schiller Park, located in the historic German Village neighborhood south of downtown Columbus, is one of the most scenic and social parks in the city. Hiding among the towering oak trees that offer summer shade to picnickers and dog walkers is a royal secret.

A pin oak tree located on the grounds, called the "Peace Oak," has significant ties to Columbus's only known royal wedding. The tree that has that designation now is a replacement for the original that died in 2004.

The tree was dedicated in 1871 during the wedding of Amelia May Parsons and Prince Ernst Manderup Alexander zu Lynar of Prussia. The romantic story of a Columbus woman who fell in love with a prince and then returned to her hometown to wed made international headlines and put Columbus in the spotlight.

The tree planting had nothing to do with the wedding other than convenient timing. It commemorated the end of the Franco-Prussian War and was simply a peace

---

The pin oak tree, like the one planted during Columbus's only known royal wedding ceremony, is one the most popular shade trees native to the Midwest. Its symmetrical structure and sweeping lower branches make it ideal for park settings.

The replacement Peace Oak stands behind the lamppost that stands diagonally in line with the indented ground where the original tree once stood.

THE PEACE OAK

WHAT A tree with ties to the only known royal wedding in Columbus history

WHERE Alongside a path on the north side of Schiller Park in German Village on Reinhard Ave.

COST None

PRO TIP There are no markers on the site of the original pin oak tree or the replacement tree, so you will have to look closely for the indentation in the ground from the original stump and work your way southwest to identify the current tree.

celebration in German Village that happened to be scheduled during the Prince's visit. With no plaque to identify its significance, the tree became more associated with the royal wedding than with the war.

Very few people know where the original tree was, or where the replacement is, because of its understated past and lack of markings. To find it, start at the walking path located halfway along Reinhard Avenue and proceed to the first street lamp on the right. The large pin oak behind it is the replacement Peace Oak planted in 2000. Located diagonally across the path from the pin oak is a large round indentation in the grass which is the only indicator of the location of the original tree.

COLUMBUS PARK OF ROSES

WHAT A spectacular public garden featuring more than 12,000 roses

WHERE 3901 N High St.

COST None

PRO TIP The best time to visit the park is mid-June through mid-September when the roses are in full bloom.

Where do thousands of roses bloom in secluded gardens?

The Columbus Park of Roses is one of the most spectacular yet underappreciated sanctuaries in the city. The park and public paths are tucked away at the end of a dead-end roadway behind the Columbus Metropolitan Library Whetstone Branch in north Columbus.

The Park of Roses is just one section of a large recreational area at Whetstone Park. The gardens are sectioned into collections that feature more than twelve thousand roses and flowers. Among the blooms are rare roses and some exotic varieties.

The Formal Rose Garden features hybrid teas, shrub roses, and other modern roses, while the Heritage Rose Garden is designed with old roses like gallicas and species that only bloom once a year. There is an herb garden in the park, a perennial garden, and the Earth-Kind Rose Garden, which showcases commercial roses grown with no pesticides, fertilizers, or pruning.

What started with two thousand tea roses planted in 1952 on thirteen acres of land bloomed into the largest rose

More than four hundred varieties of roses make up the gardens at the Columbus Park of Roses.

Top left: One of hundreds of rose bush varieties at the Park of Roses.

Top right: View of the Park of Roses from an elevated gazebo.

Bottom right: Entrance to the Columbus Park of Roses

Bottom left: Rose trellises decorate the Park of Roses, which is a popular place for weddings.

garden in the world owned by a city. The American Rose Society originally occupied the land during a search for a location to showcase America's best roses. The move put Columbus on the map as the Rose Capital of America.

After years of adding new varieties and a community commitment to the garden, it remained a special sanctuary even after the American Rose Society left. The public park now includes memorial park benches, fountains, and a lookout tower. It is a popular park for weddings, photographs, and quiet meditation.

MAGIC BEYOND THE GRAVE

What famous magician keeps watch on Columbus from the grave?

Many people drive by the Green Lawn Abbey mausoleum on the small road leading to Columbus's largest graveyard, Green Lawn Cemetery, but most have no idea what that grand structure is that sits high on the hill. Behind the elegant walls, intricate stained-glass windows, and barred doorways is the final resting place for internationally renowned magician Howard Thurston. Thurston was a Columbus native who became the lifelong rival of the famous magician Harry Houdini.

Both magicians rose to stardom in the 1920s, one-upping each other with more extreme and daring acts throughout their entire careers. Upon his deathbed Thurston vowed to return from the grave as his ultimate act, but Columbus still awaits his promised return.

Thurston was born in Columbus in 1869 and captured international attention by perfecting his grand illusions for audiences. Both Thurston and Houdini got their start as small-town magicians, making a name for themselves by pushing the limits of illusion. While Houdini became known as an escape artist, Thurston focused on elaborate stage performances and special effects.

Howard Thurston caught the magic bug while skipping school one day to watch a French magician perform and ending up as an audience volunteer during one of the acts.

Green Lawn Abbey, where magician Howard Thurston is entombed.

Some of Thurston's most popular acts included the floating lady in "Amazement" and the "Sawing in Half," an illusion in which he cut his assistant in two. One of Thurston's most famous acts was making a woman vanish in "The Wonder Show of the Universe," performed at the High Street Theater.

Thurston's performance signature was over-the-top theatrics and sensory experiences like gunshots that made showgirls disappear.

After Thurston died in 1936 his body lay in rest at the Green Lawn Abbey mausoleum. Thurston never ceased to amaze audiences with astounding acts, which is one reason many people believe that the magician will someday make good on his promise to return from the grave.

GREEN LAWN ABBEY MASOLEUM

WHAT Magician Howard Thurston entombed in the Green Lawn Abbey mausoleum

WHERE 700 Greenlawn Ave. on top of the hill

COST None

PRO TIP Due to vandalism, the Green Lawn Abbey is almost never open, but you can walk up to the building and look through the bars. The Green Lawn Abbey Preservation Association opens the Abbey to the public during limited hours on Memorial Day and when hosting special events.

58 HIDDEN CIVIL WAR CEMETERY

Where do thousands of cars unknowingly pass a historical treasure every day?

It would seem that a historically significant spot in Columbus that sits on a busy roadway with thousands of cars passing daily would be well-known in the city. But the tiny Camp Chase Confederate Cemetery on Sullivant Avenue is relatively unknown, even to many Columbus natives.

The inconspicuous cemetery seems randomly placed on this site set back from the roadway in the Hilltop area. Despite its quiet presence, it is the largest northern Confederate Cemetery, with twenty-two hundred people buried there.

Camp Chase served as a military staging, training, and prison camp between 1861 and 1865 during the American Civil War. The property originated as a Union army camp before transitioning into a prison for Confederate soldiers. It was designed to hold two thousand prisoners, but by 1864 more than eight thousand were housed there. By the

CAMP CHASE CONFEDERATE CEMETERY

WHAT The final resting place of more than twenty-two hundred Civil War soldiers

WHERE 2900 Sullivant Ave.

COST None

PRO TIP Camp Chase is listed on the National Register of Historic Places.

Every June, the Hilltop Historical Society holds a memorial service to honor the military service members at Camp Chase Cemetery.

Monument among the graves at Camp Chase Confederate Cemetery.

Inset: The gates to Camp Chase visible from Sullivant Avenue.

time it closed in 1865, the number of Confederate prisoners incarcerated in Camp Chase had swelled to more than twenty-six thousand.

Over that short span of time, the overcrowding led to unsanitary conditions resulting in malnutrition, disease, and death. The Camp Chase Cemetery was built in 1863 to accommodate the increasing volume of dying prisoners.

For nearly twenty years after the camp closed, the land and the cemetery sat neglected. Congress appropriated money to build a stone wall around the cemetery in 1886, but it would be another decade before a former Union soldier named William Knauss cleaned up the grounds to provide a proper resting place for the dead.

Knauss held the first Memorial Day service at Camp Chase Cemetery in 1895 and began an effort to add monuments to the grounds honoring all the American soldiers buried there.

It is hard to believe that fewer than two acres of land in Columbus holds this much history. It is a small treasure worthy of a second look for the commuters who normally speed by it on Sullivant Avenue.

Where is there a forgotten pet cemetery in Columbus?

From Sawyer Road, the Brown Pet Cemetery looks like a human cemetery, barely visible behind the extensive overgrowth of trees and shrubs. Although the pet cemetery no longer accepts burials, a stroll through the three acres reveals a menagerie of headstones, decorative grave markers, and memorial tributes that exemplify the unbreakable bond between pets and their owners.

Elaborate headstone of tabby cat Corinna Shively in the abandoned Brown Pet Cemetery

"Faithful and loving pets: Memories that time cannot erase," says one of the headstones for Junior and Nipper, who died two years apart in the 1970s. A tiny headstone etched with flowers memorializes Beki, a poodle that died at the age of three. And then there is the inscribed headstone for Corinna Shively, a beloved cat with both a first and last name. In a headstone photo, she dons an exotic headdress signifying her elite status.

More than one thousand headstones, sectioned by decades, are scattered among the grounds, with the earliest dating back to 1925. The memorials range from simplistic hand-carved wooden headstones and metal plates to homemade stone-inlayed concrete and elaborate laser-engraved granite.

The touching tributes to Coco, Fluffy, Skeeter, Tiny, Lil' Abner, Mitzi Poo, Duke, Toodles, Trixie, and others

Pet headstones scattered and uncared for in the Brown Pet Cemetery.

Inset: The only marker showing the name of the Brown Pet Cemetery, barely visible from the roadway.

are gentle reminders of how much pets are a part of the family. There are even tributes to "Lassie" and a "Rin-Tin," providing insight into some of the decades that these pets lived, without even looking at the dates on the headstones.

The lack of upkeep to the cemetery adds to the poignancy of this forgotten place that protects the treasured memories of pets and their owners.

THE BROWN PET CEMETERY

WHAT Abandoned pet cemetery

WHERE 5013 Sawyer Rd., behind the John Glenn Columbus International Airport and nearly across from the 94th Aero Squadron restaurant

COST None

PRO TIP The marker at the entrance is an engraved rock covered by an overgrown tree.

The Brown Pet Cemetery was founded by local veterinarian Walter A. Brown. Among the burials are dogs, cats, ducks, and even a parakeet.

60

CONCRETE CORN

Where are there cement corn stalks on old farmland and why?

Although it is not unusual to spot fields of corn growing in some Columbus suburbs, most people do not expect to see larger-than-life cement versions of the favorite Ohio produce along the roadside.

A small field just off Rings Road in the heart of a business park in Dublin features 109 concrete ears of corn. Each ear is six feet three inches tall placed in rows on a plot of farmland that once belonged to a prominent agriculturalist.

The Field of Corn (with Osage Oranges) is an art installation project erected by the Dublin Art in Public Places program of the Dublin Arts Council. Artist Malcolm Cochran designed the spectacle that often catches drivers off guard.

While the Osage oranges get recognition in the project's name, they are not a part of the artistic design. Instead, the reference pays homage to the natural trees that line the property, serving as a backdrop to the ears of corn.

FIELD OF CORN (WITH OSAGE ORANGES)

WHAT Giant concrete corn statues in the middle of a Dublin business park

WHERE 4995 Rings Rd., Dublin

COST None

PRO TIP You will not find a single matching kernel pattern on any two ears of corn. This is a deliberate detail by the artist.

Each ear of corn in the Field of Corn (with Osage Oranges) weighs fifteen hundred pounds.

The Field of Corn statues alongside the roadway in a Dublin corporate park.

Inset: One of 109 larger-than-life ears of corn in the Dublin suburb.

Local farmer Sam Frantz tended that plot of land from 1935 to 1967 and was instrumental in the creation of hybrid corn. Though merely a coincidence that this land was selected for the project, the Field of Corn artwork is a fitting tribute to Frantz. The site is now called Frantz Park. The Frantz family was on hand during the sculpture dedication in 1994.

The site is unknown to many due to its secluded location, but it is a pleasant surprise for those who catch a glimpse of it on the Dublin side street.

61

REMNANTS OF AVIATION HISTORY

Where is the original terminal for Port Columbus?

Before the Columbus airport was the John Glenn Columbus International Airport, it was Port Columbus. And before the control tower facilitated air traffic from International Gateway, it managed incoming and outgoing flights from East Fifth Avenue.

While the times have changed for airline passengers in Columbus, the original terminal and control tower is a pillar of forgotten of aviation history. If not for its extensive historical significance, the building might have already been demolished.

The now dilapidated building has seen its share of notable aviation figures since it was built in 1920. The inauguration ceremony at the terminal on July 8, 1929, signified two aviation milestones. It was the beginning of air transportation in Columbus and the site connecting the first transcontinental-rail voyages.

Columbus was the crossover for passengers traveling from New York to Los Angeles by rail and plane on the Transcontinental Air Transport. Passengers took a series of trains and planes during a forty-eight-hour voyage from New York to Columbus to Waynoka, Oklahoma, and Clovis, New Mexico, before arriving in L.A.

OLD PORT COLUMBUS TERMINAL AND CONTROL TOWER

WHAT The abandoned original terminal and control tower for Port Columbus that was built in 1920

WHERE 4920 E Fifth Ave.

COST None

PRO TIP The old building is a treasure but only available to view from the exterior. Exercise care because the area surrounding it is isolated.

Original control tower for Port Columbus sitting abandoned on the fringe of the airport.

That inaugural celebration at the terminal brought in transportation pioneers like Henry Ford and aviation trailblazers, Charles Lindbergh and Amelia Earhart.

The run-down and empty terminal now sits on the fringe of the John Glenn Columbus International Airport. The silent lots surrounding the building are abandoned and covered with weeds. In recent years, efforts have been made to preserve the structure, but it currently sits unused.

The control tower still features original equipment visible from the outside. The Art Deco architecture has a rustic flare with a tone of elegance, making it easy to imagine it as a landmark for passengers and pilots returning home to Columbus after a long flight. The tower's understated elegance probably lent itself to aviation celebrations for visiting dignitaries in the 1920s.

The original airport terminal spent time on the Columbus Landmarks Foundation's "Most Endangered Buildings List" that spotlights notable historic buildings in danger of irreparable damage or demolition.

62

LONE SKYSCRAPER

What downtown building was the only skyscraper in Columbus for half a century?

The downtown city skyline is spectacular, especially as a backdrop for the developing Scioto riverfront area. That is why it is hard to believe that for fifty-two years the LeVeque Tower was the only skyscraper in Columbus.

Built in 1927, the LeVeque Tower was originally used for the expanding American Insurance Union (AIU Citadel), an insurance company that doubled as a secret society and a popular social element in the early 1900s. AIU membership included secret handshakes, signals, and society initiations. The society outgrew its original headquarters at Front and Broad Streets and needed a new building for its growing business and social endeavors.

The forty-seven-story building was designed to be 555.5 feet tall, five inches taller than the Washington Monument. The skyscraper was the tallest building between New York and Chicago at the time of construction. It was Columbus's first and only skyscraper.

The upper floors of the LeVeque Tower that stood as Columbus's only skyscraper for fifty-two years.

Though no longer the tallest skyscraper in Columbus, the LeVeque Tower is still the most distinctive building downtown.

The LeVeque Tower is one of the most recognizable landmarks in the downtown skyline.

THE LEVEQUE TOWER

WHAT The first skyscraper in Columbus

WHERE 50 W Broad St.

COST None

PRO TIP The best view of the LeVeque Tower is at night when the upper stories are illuminated.

It would remain that way until 1977 when the Rhodes State Office Tower joined the downtown landscape, surpassing the AIU at 629 feet tall.

When the Great Depression took its toll on the AIU in the 1930s, the building was acquired by the LeVeque family. The name changed to the LeVeque Tower, starting a new era for its presence in downtown Columbus.

Renovations through the decades have modified the building from office space to residences and most recently a grand hotel that occupies some of the floors. Through all of its evolutions the building retained its original Art Deco charm.

The exterior lights on the upper stories of the tower, originally installed to alert airplanes flying near the city, are now used to illuminate the building with various colors throughout the year, commemorating events like the Fourth of July in red, white, and blue and changing to pink for Breast Cancer Awareness Month in October.

63 COLUMBUS—BIKE FRIENDLY BEFORE IT WAS COOL

Why are there so many bikes and bike paths around the city?

Lots of cities are going green and getting healthy by jumping onto the bike-friendly bandwagon. Columbus is no different, except that the city was bike-friendly almost 150 years before it was a key initiative in other major cities around the United States.

The City of Columbus organized the first official bicycle club in 1872, with fewer than twenty members the first year. While informal groups already existed for bicycle enthusiasts, the official Columbus Bicycle Club gave the initiative new momentum. Members participated in organized rides, like the popular ten mile ride to Shadesville, Ohio, and other destinations around the state. The club grew every year, with several hundred members pedaling together by 1883.

Cycling fever has never left the city. The modern-day emphasis on getting around on two-wheels only provides more resources for what was already an important mode of transportation and leisure sport in Columbus.

Today, bike rental stations in downtown make getting around easy. CoGo Bike Share has 365 bikes available for anyone to rent and forty-six bicycle stations throughout the downtown area.

Beyond downtown there is a sixty-five-mile, off-road network of bicycle trails that connect to the suburbs. The Olentangy Trail that starts in Worthington and the twenty-two-mile Alum Creek trail are two of the most popular.

A bike rental location in downtown Columbus.

Inset: Bicyclist in downtown Columbus.

Columbus continues to cater to bicyclists, with dedicated bike lanes, extensive bike parking options, and bike racks on COTA buses for those with longer commutes. The Mid-Ohio Regional Planning Commission (MORPC) publishes regularly updated maps of current bike trails online.

BICYCLES IN COLUMBUS

WHAT The bike-friendly commitment throughout the city

WHERE Everywhere in downtown Columbus and its suburbs

COST Rent a CoGo bike for $18 for a three-day pass or ride your own.

PRO TIP Many Columbus suburbs have their own bicycle clubs that you can join.

The Scioto Trail that runs along the downtown riverfront is one of the most scenic bike paths in Columbus, with a front-row view of the downtown skyline.

64 SCOTTISH SOUNDS IN THE NEIGHBORHOOD

Where can I hear the sound of bagpipes coming from a residential neighborhood?

Calumet Street in north Columbus runs through quiet residential neighborhoods, but Tuesday nights are infused with an elegant international ambiance. The hypnotic sounds of Scottish bagpipes often echo from St. James Episcopal Church, where the Capital City Pipes & Drums band practices every week.

While the group mostly practices inside the church, there are times when they practice marching formations outside and draw an impromptu audience with an alluring call to the ears similar to the way the smell of baking bread calls to the nose. Families and dog walkers out for a stroll cannot help but congregate and listen to the romantic sounds coming from the bagpipes.

The best opportunity to enjoy this spontaneous performance is on Tuesday evenings before major holidays,

CAPITAL CITY PIPES & DRUMS

WHAT The oldest pipe band in the city, playing Scottish music at events and during weekly practices in north Columbus

WHERE St. James Episcopal Church on Calumet St.

COST None

PRO TIP You can check the Capital City Pipes & Drums website for upcoming event appearances.

Learning to play the bagpipes requires a commitment of at least thirty minutes of practice per day.

Capital City Pipes & Drums preparing for a performance at the Dublin Irish Festival.

Inset: Tuesday night practices for Capital City Pipes & Drums at St. James Episcopal Church.

including community parades or before major city events where the group is performing.

Capital City Pipes & Drums was formed by a Scotsman named Bobby Peters who immigrated to Columbus in 1923 with a passion to teach the sounds of his homeland to residents in his new community. The group formed in 1963 and remains the oldest and longest ongoing pipe band in Central Ohio.

Peters died in 1984, but his gift of Celtic music to Columbus continues.

The sounds of the Scottish Highlands resonate throughout Columbus at weddings, funerals, and parades. Capital City Pipes & Drums is always featured at the Dublin Irish Festival. The group participates globally in pipe band competitions, so catching a glimpse of the group during a practice is a treat for anyone who is passing by.

65 FEED SACK FLARE

THE NORTH MARKET

WHAT A marketplace for local vendors selling artisanal food, art, spices, flowers, and unique goods

WHERE 59 Spruce St. in downtown Columbus

COST Free to browse but you will likely end up buying something

PRO TIP If you are dining at the North Market, it is best to take a full lap around the place to consider the wide variety of food options before making a commitment. Be sure to get your parking lot ticket validated from a vendor for the cheaper parking rate.

What iconic logo in Columbus was influenced by a feed sack?

No visit to Columbus is complete without a stop at the North Market in downtown where local vendors sell everything from meat and baked goods to flowers, spices, and cheese. The North Market logo featuring a colorful rooster as its centerpiece is one of the most recognized logos in the city. While the symbol captures the essence of the North Market perfectly, the design is derived from an old feed sack that someone picked up by chance.

The discarded sack was left behind in the Quonset hut that served as the second home for the North Market from 1948 to 1995. During a design competition in 1995 someone found the discarded cloth sack and used it as creative inspiration for their logo submission. The rooster has become synonymous with the market ever

The landscape at the North Market will change by 2020 with the construction of a thirty-five-story mixed-use Market Tower and public plaza.

North Market: The modern-day North Market.

Inset: North Market shoppers peruse local products for sale by vendors.

Left: The original feed sack that was the inspiration for the North Market logo.

since. The original feed sack was preserved and is now framed and hanging on the second floor of the North Market outside of the administrative offices.

This bit of history represents one of the longest-standing public markets in Columbus. The original North Market was one of four in the city, opening as the North End Market in 1876. When that burned to the ground in 1948, the Quonset hut became a temporary second space until the North Market and its merchants moved into the current space on Spruce Street in 1995. The building comprises two warehouses from the 1800s, adding to the rustic local feel that embraces Columbus's history.

LUSTRON HOMES

Why are there random homes in Columbus that do not match anything around them?

It is not unusual to see various styles of home architecture throughout Columbus, but Lustron homes stand out because most people do not know exactly what to call them. The uniquely sterile and utilitarian appearance of a Lustron home is unmistakable. There are not many left in Columbus, which makes their presence in neighborhoods even more noteworthy because they appear so randomly placed. There are several in the Clintonville area and on the east side of Columbus.

Lustron homes cropped up in Columbus after World War II as a quick response to housing needs for returning veterans. The former Lustron Corporation was based in Columbus near the airport where it mass-produced durable enameled steel homes at affordable prices to serve Columbus's housing shortage in the 1940s.

The efficient, industrial, one-story homes are constructed of porcelain steel that keeps radiant heat inside and allows for simple maintenance. They are easy to wash with a hose and pictures hang on the walls with magnets. There are built-in

LUSTRON HOMES

WHAT Efficient enameled steel homes mass-produced in the 1940s to serve a housing shortage

WHERE A few of the remaining Lustron homes are in parts of Clintonville on Arden, Weisheimer, and Kanawha and on the east side of Columbus. The Ohio History Connection features a Lustron home in its collection, but it is not clear how long the structure will remain with the facility.

COST None

PRO TIP The Lustron Company produced only twenty-five hundred homes.

One of a few original Lustron Homes still occupied in Columbus neighborhoods.

kitchen cabinets and bookshelves for storage, and an open floor plan makes the homes flexible and comfortable. Some models even include a combo dishwasher and washing machine called the "Automagic," providing homeowners with an even more efficient lifestyle.

There are several models of Lustron homes, ranging from the 713-square-foot, two-bedroom "Meadowbrook" to the 1,140-square-foot, three-bedroom "Weschester Deluxe."

All Lustron homes are ranch-style, with steel panels that bolt onto a concrete slab. The inside steel is embossed to look like wood paneling. Lustron engineer Carl Strandlund claimed that the homes could withstand fire, rust, decay, and damage from vermin and termites. The promised longevity of the home's structure is perhaps why a few them still stand in Columbus neighborhoods looking exactly the way they did in 1948.

Lustron homes originally sold for between $8,500 and $9,500.

Where is the highest elevation in downtown Columbus?

Chances are, despite researching Columbus records, those who are looking for a marker of the city's highest elevation point are not going to find it.

The highest elevation in Columbus is located on the fringe of the King-Lincoln District in the front yard of St. Paul African Methodist Episcopal Church. That is a different location from where the official marker for Columbus's highest elevation stood for decades.

The marker was once placed in the northeast corner of the former Franklin County courthouse, located at South High Street and East Fulton. The courthouse was demolished in 1974 to make way for a new twenty-seven-story courthouse across the street. After the courthouse was razed, the corner of the block became the public space now known as Dorrian Commons Park.

Although the former courthouse housed the marker for the highest elevation in downtown Columbus, the altitude of the location is 770 feet. Only the Statehouse has a higher elevation, at 775 feet. Both locations are still shy of what current Franklin County records show as the highest point in downtown Columbus, at St. Paul AME Church, which is 799 feet above sea level, bounded by I-670, I-70, I-71, and State Route 315.

While no one knows what happened to the official elevation marker since the demolition of the original courthouse, it is curious that is was never the highest elevation in downtown to begin with when the marker was originally placed.

St. Paul AME Church in downtown Columbus, with the city's highest elevation in the front yard.

The St. Paul AME Church was completed in 1906 to accommodate a growing congregation on a plot of land that current county engineers identify as the highest elevation in downtown Columbus.

ST. PAUL AFRICAN METHODIST EPISCOPAL CHURCH

WHAT Highest elevation in downtown Columbus

WHERE 639 E Long St. in the southeast corner of the front yard

COST None

PRO TIP St. Paul A.M.E. Church is the oldest congregation of African descent in Columbus, organized in 1823.

68

ROAD TO NOWHERE

Where is there an abandoned section of freeway overlooking the city skyline?

One of the most perplexing hidden treasures in Columbus is an abandoned and elevated section of freeway over I-70 West in downtown. The stillness that lingers on the forgotten and unfinished stretch of roadway could easily serve as the backdrop for an apocalyptic zombie movie.

The weeds growing through the cracks of the faded blacktop, stark graffiti on the highway edges, and the abrupt stop on each end of the section make it a surprising find. The yellow dividing lines indicate that the road had purpose at one point, or at least good intentions, but few people beyond the homeless who live near there even know it exists. Drivers pass right under it during their morning commute.

The section of freeway is located between the Scioto Audubon Metropark in the Brewery District and the Scioto Mile bicycle and walking path along the downtown riverfront. The section of roadway is not easy to spot from its elevated position over I-70 West hovering above railroad tracks. It appears that the road was intended to connect to what is now the dead end of Mound Street, just past the Miranova tower.

The Ohio Department of Transportation anticipates the removal of the abandoned section of highway in 2020 during a reconfiguration project of the 70/71 corridor through downtown Columbus.

Abandoned and unknown section of freeway in the heart of downtown Columbus.

ABANDONED SECTION OF FREEWAY

WHAT Leftover progress that did not make the cut for future downtown development

WHERE Crossing over I-70 West in the heart of downtown between the Scioto Audubon Metropark and the Scioto Mile

COST None

PRO TIP Due to the remote location and the vast number of homeless camps in the area, do not venture to this location alone. Your best time to visit is midday.

The Columbus Engineer's Office says the section was originally designed to be a ramp from Mound Street to I-70 West. The project was abandoned when a different ramp from I-70 West was constructed at Civic Center Drive and 2nd Street just a short distance from this location.

The Ohio Department of Transportation confirms that the section of highway was closed off during the construction of Miranova in the 1990s and for the reconfiguring of streets in the area. It appears that this section of highway was never used or completed. It was just forgotten.

The added bonus of finding this section of roadway is enjoying one of the best views of the downtown skyline.

69

WHAT'S IN A NAME?

What popular Columbus park bears a name of someone almost no one knows?

Goodale Park is one of the most recognizable and frequently utilized public parks in Columbus's Short North district. While the Goodale Park name is fairly well-known, the man behind it is not. Ask anyone enjoying the walkways, benches, and peaceful pond in the park who Goodale is, and they likely do not know.

The plot of land was donated to the City of Columbus in 1851 by Dr. Lincoln Goodale, giving Columbus its very first park. He donated forty acres for the park to provide a green space in the heart of the city. The donation of forestland was intended to provide the public a special place to enjoy nature. Historians believe that Dr. Goodale wanted to preserve

GOODALE PARK

WHAT A popular community park named after a man whom few people know

WHERE 120 W Goodale in Victorian Village

COST None

PRO TIP Throughout its more than 160-year history, Goodale Park has served as a Union Army Civil War encampment; an animal park with bears, foxes, and wolves; and a meeting spot during the Temperance movement.

The newer trees planted in Goodale Park are selected to represent the personalities of those who donated money for them. Flowering trees are planted for socialite benefactors, nut trees for community characters, and oak trees for loyal contributors.

One of several decorative entrances to Goodale Park in downtown Columbus.

Inset: Statue of Lincoln Goodale in the center of Goodale Park.

this section of land from the industry developing around it. It was his way to protect the trees, flowers, birds, and hills so the community could enjoy them for years to come.

Dr. Goodale's contributions to Columbus were significant. He had a medical practice in Franklinton and became Franklin County's first doctor, in 1805. Dr. Goodale was the first millionaire in the city and one of the first prominent local philanthropists, investing in the community through business and real estate. He served as a city councilman and city recorder, and when he died in 1868 Dr. Goodale was one of the oldest residents in Ohio.

Visitors to Goodale Park can find a statue located at the south entrance honoring the man behind the name and his contributions to Columbus.

Where is Columbus's original pedestrian subway?

Columbus does not have a traditional subway, so the concept of traveling below ground in any fashion is not familiar to most city residents. That is why a pedestrian subway on North High Street that appeared in the early twentieth century is such a novelty.

A view of the stairs leading underneath High Street in the pedestrian subway.

A stretch of north High Street immediately south of East North Broadway has a pedestrian subway that looks like a bus shelter on each side of the street. It is the only such pedestrian subway in Columbus, but it was built out of necessity in 1928 after a tragic accident involving a child on his way to school.

Clinton Elementary School sits at the busy intersection of High Street and Clinton Heights Avenue. In the early 1900s no crosswalks existed to help children cross the street to school. As a result, a young boy was hit by a street car and lost his leg. The incident brought new awareness to the community of the dangers that children face just getting to class.

The suburb of Dublin built a similar pedestrian underpass beneath Riverside Drive in 2016.

Pedestrian subway outside of Clinton Elementary School.

Local business professionals in the Clintonville area pooled money to build the pedestrian subway to provide the kids with safe passage to school. While this was the only pedestrian subway in the Columbus area for more than eighty-five years, some city suburbs are now looking into similar concepts as vehicle congestion increases and traffic patterns change.

PEDESTRIAN SUBWAY

WHAT The original pedestrian subway

WHERE High St. between E North Broadway and Clinton Heights Ave.

COST None

PRO TIP The pedestrian subway entrance is sometimes locked, but you can still peer down through the bars to see the tunnel that crosses to the other side of the street.

71

CREATIVE SPACE

Where is the most inspirational elevator in Columbus?

Most elevators could use a conversation piece to spur close-quarter interaction, but one elevator in Columbus has no problem inspiring those who step inside. The "ArtOvater" in the Columbus Cultural Arts Center downtown houses an eclectic collection of sketches, stickers, messages, and artwork ranging from a single pink flower to a pen-drawn skeleton character that consumes half a wall.

Those who ride the elevator from the first to the third floor get a good twenty seconds to add their own artful reflection of the moment to the walls of the ArtOvater. In fact, any kind of artistic expression is encouraged, including dancing.

The center created the ArtOvater as an experiment during the 2017 Columbus Arts Festival to give people something to do on the slow elevator ride to the third-floor Loft Gallery. The music

COLUMBUS CULTURAL ARTS CENTER

WHAT Visual arts center for adult classes and exhibits, with a secret inspirational elevator

WHERE 139 W Main St.

COST Free to visit exhibits and ride the elevator

PRO TIP If you are feeling extra inspired, the Cultural Arts Center holds classes throughout the year on everything from ceramics and painting to weaving and printmaking.

For more than forty years the Cultural Arts Center has provided visual art opportunities to adults in the Columbus community.

A sensory experience awaits inside the ArtOVater from one floor to the next.

pumped into the small space comes from DJ mixtapes left over from weddings held at the building.

It turns out the ArtOvater provided more inspiration than was ever expected. The experiment was such a success that the center now invites local artists to apply periodically and develop their own creative interpretation of the space.

The Cultural Arts Center, in the River South district across from Bicentennial Park downtown, is the city's visual arts center and gallery featuring local and emerging artists who specialize in a wide variety of media. The Columbus Cultural Arts Center was originally an Ohio State Arsenal in 1861, serving as a weapons storage facility until the Columbus Recreation and Parks Department found a new—artistic—vision for it in 1973.

72

PATRIOTIC ROCK

Where is the most interesting rock in Columbus?

FRANKLINTON CENTENNIAL ROCK

WHAT A large boulder commemorating the centennial celebration of the Franklinton neighborhood in 1897

WHERE Turn right on Lechner off W. Broad Street. Drive past the Ohio Department of Public Safety complex to the north end of the road. Follow the paved path to the left for about a half mile to the dead end. Look to the left in the brush and you will see the tip of the boulder slightly above the weeds and cattails.

COST None

PRO TIP The area is fairly secluded, so it is advised not to search for the rock alone.

Columbus has a number of quarries, so interesting rocks and large boulders are not a novelty around the city, except for one.

A colossal boulder with a fifty-one-foot circumference lies mostly hidden in the bushes and weeds near the Ohio Department of Public Safety complex on West Broad Street. The glacial rock was once a proud landmark for the Franklinton community.

The boulder was the centerpiece of an elaborate centennial celebration in the village of Franklinton in 1897. At the time, village leaders wanted to create a celebration so grand to honor the area's one-hundred-year history that it would be noted in history books. The celebration was a gathering for settlers to present songs and speeches paying homage to Lucas Sullivant, who founded the village. There were parades, fireworks, and flag-raising ceremonies with

The Franklinton Centennial Rock is one of the largest glacial boulders in the area.

Top left: The Centennial Rock in Franklinton as it was displayed during the 1897 centennial celebration. Credit: Franklinton Historical Society.

Top right: Current state of the Centennial Rock, which appears to be the same side of the rock in the historic photograph.

Bottom left: Present-day Centennial Rock hidden among trees and overgrown grass.

Bottom right: The Centennial Rock is hidden behind tall weeds and grass off the dead end of a walking path.

hundreds of volunteers and participants. Franklinton was and still is a proud community.

The boulder was painted for the grand event, and there was a marquee for photographs. Had Instagram existed in the nineteenth century, Franklinton boulder selfies would have gone viral.

After the celebration, the painted boulder became a proud and prominent landmark for the Franklinton community. The century that followed came with urban development that eventually swallowed the land surrounding it and the boulder disappeared into tall brush and cattails.

The boulder is not an easy find—especially when compared with the historical photo—but an exciting one. Unfortunately, graffiti and mother nature have erased all of the original markings from the rock, but there is still space around it that provides a sense of its historical significance.

73

OSU'S NON-FRATERNITY FRATERNITY

Why is an unofficial fraternity so renowned in OSU's history?

It does not take much of a drive through The Ohio State University campus to realize how instrumental Greek life is to the social element of the university.

One of the oldest fraternities at the school started as a joke, but it has since become a centerpiece for tight friendships. The unofficial fraternity of SI-U had no charter, no house, no song, and no dues or officers. In fact, they never even held an official meeting. The one thing that the SI-U fraternity did have was solid friendships and some famous recruits, including Jesse Owens and James Rhodes, who eventually became governor of Ohio.

SI-U members designated Smitty's Drug Store at 16th and High Streets as its international headquarters and chapter house. The unofficial meetings of the unofficial fraternity took place on the bar stools at Smitty's and in the basement of Bob Hill's Tailoring shop. In 1932, during the Great Depression, Smitty's became a popular hangout, especially for OSU athletes. It was a common spot for conversation about the one thing they all had in common, a lack of money.

By 1957, the bond of friendship exploded, and then-current members decided to hold an unofficial SI-U reunion. More than two hundred alumni showed up. The alumni reunions honor notable names as a result of sharing bar

The SI-U fraternity used beer caps as the pledge pins for their unofficial charter.

Construction at the corner of 16th & High Street on campus where the SI-U fraternity used to hang out at Smitty's Drug Store.

NON-FRATERNITY HEADQUARTERS

WHAT International headquarters for OSU's unofficial fraternity SI-U during the Great Depression

WHERE Corner of 16th & High Sts. Smitty's Drug Store is no longer there, and the area is under construction.

COST None

PRO TIP OSU has more than seventy fraternities and sororities represented on campus, some with official housing on Greek Row.

stools, stories, and handshakes. Honorees have included Jack Nicklaus, cartoonist Milton Caniff, Senator Bill Saxbe, and OSU basketball player Jimmy Hull, who led the Buckeyes to the first-ever NCAA basketball championship game. During a biennial reunion in 1983 honoring Woody Hayes, more than three hundred alumni attended.

Smitty's Drug Store and the bonding bar stools are long gone at the corner of 16th and High. The location has undergone a number of renovations since.

⁷⁴ LOST CAPITOL CORNERSTONE

How do you lose a massive cornerstone to the Ohio Statehouse for a century and a half?

One of the most important and symbolic elements of a state's capitol building is its cornerstone. It sets the placement for all other stones that will be used around it and oftentimes serves as a time capsule, holding mementoes that were deemed significant at the date of construction.

It seems unlikely that such an important piece of masonry could be misplaced, but that is what happened to the cornerstone for the Ohio Statehouse in downtown Columbus. It went missing for nearly 150 years. Keep in mind, this cornerstone was a half-ton section of limestone.

What happened?

Official construction on the Ohio Statehouse broke ground in 1839 with a ceremonial laying of the cornerstone. Prisoners were utilized for much of the initial construction, but labor disputes and slow progress brought the entire project to a halt in 1840.

During an eight-year construction hiatus, nothing happened. So when construction got under way again, the building plans, materials, workers, and leadership had all changed. The Ohio Statehouse foundation and ground floors were already completed when crews started on the walls in

---

Much of the Statehouse, including the lost cornerstone, was built with Columbus limestone collected from the Scioto River.

The Ohio Statehouse in downtown Columbus.

OHIO STATEHOUSE CORNERSTONE

WHAT The unknown whereabouts of the Ohio Statehouse cornerstone for 150 years

WHERE Capitol Square in downtown Columbus

COST None

PRO TIP Free guided tours of the Ohio Statehouse are offered every day of the week.

1850, so no one was looking for the cornerstone at that time.

The Statehouse was finally completed in 1861. The cupola was the only uncompleted element, but the start of the Civil War put that project on hold. The three-year, $300,000 Statehouse project became a twenty-two-year monstrosity costing more than $2,000,000.

By the time it was finally completed, no one knew for sure the location of the cornerstone. It was finally rediscovered during Statehouse renovations in 1990.

Where is there a painted brick in obvious view that most people miss?

Exposed brick in renovated buildings is all the rage for adding rustic flare to modern establishments, but one

small brick in a tiny café in downtown Columbus is a bit of a curiosity.

Most patrons walk into the Brioso Roastery and Coffee Bar on East Long Street, order their specialty coffee, and relax, read, or engage in networking or business meetings. They might make note of the vintage ambiance of exposed brick on the interior walls from what was the former Faith Mission building. Most people never look close enough to discover that one single brick is different from all the rest. One brick in the wall is an elegantly painted miniature work of art hidden next to the window in the annexed seating room.

Owner Jeff Davis says many regulars sit near the brick and never even notice it until, one day, they step out of their focused state long enough to discover the artistic surprise.

Brioso Roastery showcases renovated exposed brick, which makes the hidden painted brick inside a rare find.

The hidden painted brick in Brioso Roastery is an appropriate nod to the café's location in Columbus's artsy Discovery District.

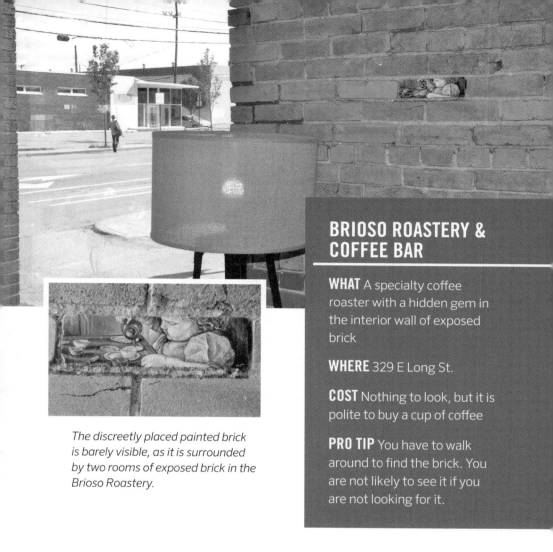

BRIOSO ROASTERY & COFFEE BAR

WHAT A specialty coffee roaster with a hidden gem in the interior wall of exposed brick

WHERE 329 E Long St.

COST Nothing to look, but it is polite to buy a cup of coffee

PRO TIP You have to walk around to find the brick. You are not likely to see it if you are not looking for it.

The discreetly placed painted brick is barely visible, as it is surrounded by two rooms of exposed brick in the Brioso Roastery.

The painted brick fittingly depicts a young girl pouring tea into a small teacup. The intricately detailed work has a 3-D effect. It was created by local street artist Mandi Caskey, who has a passion for creating art in public spaces to spur conversation.

The Brioso Roastery is known for its specialty production of large volumes of coffee and micro-lots. The small brick hidden in the cozy space of the specialty roaster adds a unique touch to the mood. It adds a delightful element of surprise to an outstanding cup of cappuccino.

RED-LIGHT DISTRICT VANISHES

Where was a street's name changed to disguise its past?

Grant Avenue is one of the most well-known streets in downtown Columbus—home to Grant Hospital and the Columbus Metropolitan Library. There is little evidence today to suggest the previous identity of the area that was once known as Columbus's high-end red-light district. In the early 1900s the section from Mound to Main Street housed the most expensive brothels in the city.

At the time, Grant Avenue was named Seventh Street. Part of the district's popularity came during a period of population growth in Columbus that brought with it an increase in vice districts offering an array of brothels, gambling saloons, and opium dens.

Seventh Street was one of several areas referred to as the Badlands, but it was the only one catering to the more affluent people who lived in the city. The low-rent Badlands area was along the Scioto River among factories and warehouses that were eventually transformed into commercial land.

By 1909 efforts got under way citywide to rid Columbus of vice districts, including the high-end ones. Along Seventh Street the people who lived and worked north of Main grew tired of the area's reputation and pushed the City Council for

Primo de Orient was one of the most exclusive brothels in Columbus's now all-but-vanished red-light district.

A section of Grant Avenue that was once Columbus's red-light district.

RED-LIGHT DISTRICT OF THE EARLY 1900S

WHAT The upscale vice neighborhood of the city, with no trace left of its roots

WHERE Grant Ave. between Mound and Main Sts.

COST None

PRO TIP Grant Avenue is a busy street, so your walk down memory lane in this district is best done on foot.

a new identity. They wanted to change the street name to Grant Avenue.

The effort worked, but the name change hardly eradicated the activity there or the reputation. Instead it simply gained a nickname as the Grant Avenue vice district.

Fortunately, a century of time and neighborhood renovations have gone a long way to change the purpose and perceptions of this small stretch of downtown.

Where is a primitive cabin siting among modern housing?

A stroll along East Norwich Avenue in Columbus's University District reveals a residential area used mostly for student housing, so no one would expect to find a primitive cabin sitting in the middle of it. The Beers cabin, as it is known, is a historic log cabin built in 1804 that is perched among housing and urban development that has grown up around it over the past two hundred years. One would think that such a primitive structure would stand out in a neighborhood dotted with student rental units, but somehow, the Beers cabin keeps a low profile and remains a Central Ohio treasure worth noticing.

Why is it there?

The previous site where pioneer David Beers built the cabin was on a plot of land at

THE DAVID BEERS CABIN

WHAT Authentic pioneer home in the middle of a University District neighborhood

WHERE E Norwich Ave.

COST None

PRO TIP Since the Beers cabin is occupied as a single-family dwelling it should be admired from the sidewalk as it is not open to the public.

The David Beers log cabin in the University District is the oldest known home in Columbus.

The Beers cabin in the heart of the University District neighborhood.

North High Street and Dodridge. The plain log cabin was simple and square and reportedly built with a stairway and trap door that led to a loft. Logs made of solid oak and walnut made up the 18-by-24-foot structure.

Nearly a century after its construction, the cabin was relocated to its present address on East Norwich Avenue. During the re-build a porch was added and the space expanded to 1,800 square feet, but most of the features are still original. Even some of the furniture inside is reportedly original, including tree-stump stools used for sitting by the fireplace.

The history of the Beers cabin is even more intriguing because of the story tied to the man who built it, David Beers. As a child, Beers was captured by Indians while traveling by horseback in the wilderness with his mother from New Jersey. His freedom came during a captive exchange at the end of the French and Indian War. Beers took up residence in Pennsylvania and eventually relocated to Columbus in 1802.

78

WARTIME PERFORMANCES

When did you need more than a show ticket to see an Ohio Theatre performance?

THE OHIO THEATRE

WHAT A renovated 1928 theatre that once required war bonds along with show tickets for admission

WHERE 39 E State St., in downtown Columbus

COST The price of a performance ticket

PRO TIP Each summer the Ohio Theatre transforms back into a nostalgic movie house during the CAPA Summer Movie Series, when patrons can catch everything from cult classics to cartoons on the big screen.

The Ohio Theatre in downtown Columbus is one of the most historic and beloved theaters in the city, attracting world-class acts from around the country. While most performances in the restored theater only require a show ticket, there was a time when patrons needed something more.

Before the Ohio Theater was a performance arts venue, it was a grand movie house. It was especially popular in the 1940s, serving as an entertaining distraction from World War II.

At the time, the Ohio Theatre was heavily into the war bond business, so in addition to show tickets patrons were also required to bring war bonds for admission. Patrons could not miss the heavy promotion and sale of war bonds in the theater lobby.

The popular movie house further supported war efforts by adding late night movie showings that enabled shift workers at the war plant to catch a little entertainment during such a difficult time for the country.

Patrons wait in line to watch a performance in the restored Ohio Theatre in downtown Columbus. Credit: Randall L. Schieber.

Inset: View from the stage inside the restored historic Ohio Theater. Credit: D.R. Goff.

One of the first showings with the dual entrance requirement was during a special world film premier of *My Sister Eileen* in 1942.

By 1969 the theatre had lost its luster and was at risk of demolition. The Columbus Association for the Performing Arts (CAPA) was formed to save it and restore it to its original 1928 appearance.

No war bonds are needed today to enjoy a performance at the Ohio Theatre, but the experience is a step back in time, surrounding patrons with the ambiance of an elegant movie house.

The restored Ohio Theatre hosts performances by the Columbus Symphony Orchestra, the Broadway Series, BalletMet, and Opera Columbus.

79

INVENTION HUB

Where are some of the world's most groundbreaking discoveries pioneered in Columbus?

The unassuming appearance of the Battelle campus on King Avenue is by design. The corporate office façade shields high-tech labs that produce some of the world's most groundbreaking improvements in science and technology. Only an aerial view of the complex can show the magnitude of the research facilities.

The Xerox machine is one of the many inventions from Battelle used in mainstream society. Credit: Battelle.

Battelle is the largest non-profit research and development institution in the world, providing innovations for private companies and government agencies. Battelle also manages several laboratories for the Department of Energy and the Department of Homeland Security around the country, but its genius and nucleus is in Columbus. Most of it is highly classified.

Battelle emerged in 1929 and is responsible for innovations that have changed business and social operations ever since. Examples include the development of copy technology (think Xerox), the UPC bar code, cruise control for cars, cut-resistant golf balls, airport security body scanners, nuclear research, and fiber

Battelle research is instrumental in developing vaccines for infectious diseases and creating smart technology used for biodefense.

Aerial view of the Battelle complex that is not visible from the roadway.
Credit: Battelle.

Inset: One of the most recognizable inventions by Battelle is the UPC bar code.
Credit: Battelle.

BATTELLE

WHAT One of the largest and most successful science and technology research institutions in the world

WHERE 505 King Ave.

COST None

PRO TIP Appreciate the Battelle inventions during a drive-by. It is a highly guarded facility, so you will not be allowed inside.

optics. Battelle's research also pushes military and medical boundaries with innovations like unmanned underwater vehicles, virtual reality medical devices, and the search for solutions to combatting the nation's opioid crisis.

It all started with Gordon Battelle, who left $1.5 million to start the Battelle Memorial Institute after his death in 1923. His mission was to solve world problems through science and technology while also giving back to the community. The understated genius of the life-changing inventions coming from Battelle mirror the understated physical presence of the facility.

80

MYSTERIOUSLY CLOAKED STATUE

Who is responsible for secretly cloaking a public statue?

One of the most prominent statues in Schiller Park in historic German Village is the *Umbrella Girl*. She is known as much for her peaceful presence as for her mysterious disappearing and re-appearing act that is a part of her history in the public green space. But the *Umbrella Girl* is part of another mystery. Every December, residents near the park awake one morning to find the *Umbrella Girl* dressed in a stunning red cloak.

No one knows who started the holiday ritual or who carries it on today, but it is a tradition that delights those who have come to expect it. The mystery started more than a decade ago when locals first noticed the girl dressed in a red coat with white fur trim one December morning. She has donned the cloak every December since. The *Umbrella Girl* wears the colorful cloak until after Christmas when, one morning, it is gone.

No one has ever stepped forward to claim credit for the charming gesture, instead leaving it as a quiet surprise designed to add cheer during the holidays.

The original *Umbrella Girl*, Hebe, the goddess of youth, arrived in Schiller Park in 1872 as a fountain display. In

---

The Schiller Park Umbrella Girl is sculpted wearing a German dirndl costume, which is enhanced over the holidays by the mysterious red cloak.

The Umbrella Girl *statue in Schiller Park is anonymously cloaked every holiday season.*

UMBRELLA GIRL STATUE

WHAT The statue in German Village's Schiller Park that is mysteriously cloaked every December

WHERE 1069 Jaeger St., in German Village

COST None

PRO TIP One of the best times to observe the cloaked *Umbrella Girl* is during the German Village's "Village Lights" luminary event held every December.

the 1950s the *Umbrella Girl* disappeared. Although efforts were launched to find the stolen statue, no one ever did. German Villagers missed the charm that the young girl brought to the park. Eventually, local artist Joan Wobst offered to re-sculpt the *Umbrella Girl* and donate it, using her daughter as a model.

The new *Umbrella Girl* was dedicated in 1996 and brought with her a new spirit and continued mystery by donning the December cloak.

81 SHIMMY-SHAKE

When did belly dancing become a thing in Columbus?

Belly dancing in Columbus might seem out of place given that the capital city is in the heart of Midwest agriculture and worlds away from the dance form's Middle Eastern roots. So no one would be likely to ever guess that Columbus is home to the first belly dance school in the Midwest and the longest-running belly dance school in the country.

Since 1971 Habeeba's Dance of the Arts in Grandview Heights has taught Egyptian Cabaret belly dancing. For those doing the quick math, that longevity equates to a lot of hip movement. The woman behind the studio, Habeeba, is an internationally acclaimed belly dancer, having performed in Las Vegas, the Playboy Club in Chicago, and on television shows, including *The Tonight Show with Johnny Carson*.

Habeeba endured years of sexism as a performer in the 1960s and '70s, which pushed her to promote the art of belly dance as a performance discipline with a body-positive mission. Perhaps that is why belly dancing appeals to all ages of women. Teenagers to seniors gain confidence as they bond with the dance form most identified as an expression of inherent femininity.

HABEEBA'S DANCE OF THE ARTS

WHAT The longest-running belly dance school in the United States

WHERE 1327 King Ave.

COST Class fees or $10 admission to monthly public hafla events

PRO TIP Monthly "hafla" dance parties are open to the public or drop-in classes are casual ways to test the belly dancing waters for the first time.

Intermediate belly dancing class at Habeeba's Dance of the Arts studio.

Inset: Habeeba in an elaborate belly dancing costume performing in the 1970s. Credit: Habeeba.

The growing popularity of belly dancing can be attributed to a push for new exercise regimens, a social climate for improving self-awareness and confidence, and the inclusion of belly dance moves into pop music choreography. Some women dive into belly dancing strictly out of curiosity.

Belly dance instruction varies in Columbus, ranging from Egyptian, Persian, and Greek dance to Middle Eastern "raqs" and even improvisational tribal-esque dance. Although most students take classes for the social element or exercise, there is a strong Columbus contingent of serious belly dance performers.

Sorry guys, belly dancing classes are mostly just for women, but you can catch regular performances at venues and events around the city.

There are more than a dozen dance schools in Columbus that offer belly dance instruction.

82

TIME-OUT

Where is there a "listening chair" in the middle of the woods?

The nineteen Columbus Metro Parks are designed to give residents locations to hike, picnic, and enjoy the outdoors in the quiet seclusion of the woods. Highbanks Metro Park on the city's north side helps visitors connect with nature even more with a "listening chair" tucked among the walnut, maple, and sycamore trees.

The listening chair sits in the woods at Highbanks Metro Park.

The listening chair is officially named the Nature Garden Throne. It is derived from the Native American culture and philosophy that everything is connected. When someone sits in the chair, it is an opportunity to quietly connect with the surrounding nature by listening to the wind, smelling the forest fragrance, observing wildlife, and feeling connected to the earth on a deeper level.

The vibrant blue throne with its colorful mosaic designs looks like a garden art centerpiece tucked away in the plants and flowers at the end of a small stone path. It is located in

Highbanks Metro Park has two preserved Adena Indian Mounds located along the trails within the park.

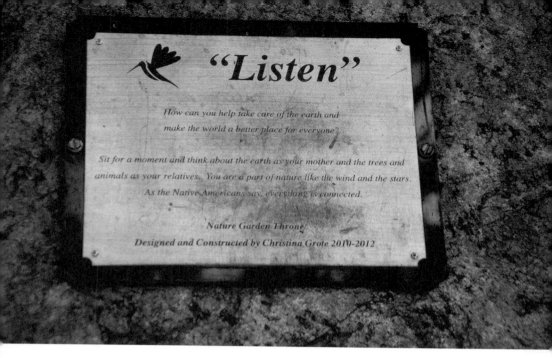

"Listen"

How can you help take care of the earth and make the world a better place for everyone?

Sit for a moment and think about the earth as your mother and the trees and animals as your relatives. You are a part of nature like the wind and the stars. As the Native Americans say, everything is connected.

Nature Garden Throne
Designed and Constructed by Christina Grote 2010-2012

The plaque on a small stone explains the importance of connecting with nature.

the woods just left of the Visitor Center at Highbanks Metro Park. Its unique presence piques curiosity, but only the observant will notice the small plaque on a rock near the chair that explains its purpose.

The message reads: "Sit for a moment and think about the earth as your mother and the trees and animals as your relatives. You are part of nature like the wind and the stars."

The chair, created by artist Christina Grote, is a fitting piece in the park due to its ties to the Adena Indians who once inhabited that land.

HIGHBANKS METRO PARK LISTENING CHAIR

WHAT An artful and elegant throne in the middle of the woods designed to connect visitors with nature

WHERE Left of the Highbanks Metro Park Visitor Center

COST None

PRO TIP To connect even more to nature after you sit in the listening chair, take a stroll on one of the trails in the park.

83

COW TOWN

One of the one hundred Jersey cows at the Waterman Dairy Farm in Columbus. Credit: Kelsie Hinds.

Where is there a working dairy farm in the middle of the city?

It is not uncommon to hear someone refer to Columbus as a cow town, but with massive downtown growth and the blurred lines between the suburbs and city there's hardly evidence that cows even existed in the capital of agricultural Ohio. For those who look hard enough, the evidence does exist. Surrounded by institutions and skyscrapers, the thriving Waterman Dairy Farm is tucked away in northwest Columbus.

The farm is part of The Ohio State University Waterman Agricultural and Natural Resources Laboratory. More than 100 Jersey cows and 160 heifers roam the thirty-seven acres of pasture, producing milk for Smith's Dairy. The farm used to supply milk to Ohio's prison system.

Columbus's dairy roots run deep. The Borden Dairy Company, with its trademark Elsie the Cow mascot, was headquartered in Columbus in the 1970s until it sold off the dairy division to Cracker Jack in 1997.

Columbus-based Ross Laboratories (now part of Abbott Laboratories) invented a milk-based baby formula in 1925—known today as Similac—and in 1973 introduced the nutritional supplement Ensure.

The American Dairy Association Mideast patented the concept of the round plastic portable bottle for milk, called the MOO KOOLER, in Columbus, revolutionizing milk's portability.

And then there is the famous butter cow sculpture

Jersey heifers on pasture at the Waterman Dairy Farm, with downtown Columbus in the background. Credit: Kelsie Hinds.

WATERMAN DAIRY FARM

WHAT A working dairy farm in the middle of Columbus

WHERE 2433 Carmack Rd., Columbus

COST None

PRO TIP Groups can book tours of the farm, but you can pet the cows through the fence if you are driving by.

that is unveiled each year at the Ohio State Fair, a tradition started in 1906. Crowds wait with bated breath in the Dairy Products Building every August for the reveal of the butter sculpture creations that have ranged from a tribute to The Ohio State Buckeyes to Darth Vader.

Visitors to Columbus who see "Cow Town" T-shirts in the airport gift shop or hear the clanking of cow bells at Columbus Clippers' baseball games might not realize that behind the metropolitan mood and newly erected skyscrapers, the city still celebrates its humble dairy roots down on the farm.

Dairy deliveries from Waterman Dairy Farm are carefully planned so as to not be delayed by morning rush hour traffic.

84

COLUMBUS CITY ANTHEM

Who knew there was one?

The city of Columbus has an official anthem. The problem is that no one knows it. That is unfortunate for the poor soul who won a contest in 1966 to create a musical tribute that residents and visitors could make synonymous with the great capital city. The song was inspired by the Scioto and Olentangy Rivers that run through Columbus.

The winning song, "Two Rivers," was selected from 103 entries and announced on a special Friday night prime-time program on WOSU-TV. The composers were Ruth Friscoe, an OSU student, and Lew Gray, an employee of WTVN radio station. The two won the $500 first prize for their ode to the city. A city council vote made "Two Rivers" Columbus's official city song.

Two Rivers
Columbus lives within two rivers
And here she tends Ohio's needs
Her voice is heard beyond those banks
To share her country's deeds.
CHORUS:
Two rivers gave her life a promise,
Two rivers fill her veins with pride.
They flow like silver ribbons thro' her hair
And they skirt her landscape wide.
So traveler pause and know these rivers
For they gave Columbus her scheme.
Perhaps they'll be your place to stand some day,
To live your life and dream.

Oddly enough, this is not the first song about Columbus. In 1947, a New York composer named Kermit Goell and lyricist Bee Walker created the song "I Had a Wonderful

The developing Scioto Mile, on the riverfront with its bike and walking paths, allows residents to enjoy the Scioto River.

COLUMBUS'S OFFICIAL CITY ANTHEM

WHAT The song "Two Rivers"

WHERE Nowhere, because no one knows it

COST N/A

PRO TIP The best way to experience the inspiration for the unknown city song is to take a stroll along the Scioto Mile, on the riverfront in downtown Columbus.

Time in Columbus." The song was connected to the housing shortage after WWII. The creators wanted the city to back an idea that would provide housing to a veteran returning from war every time the song was played on the radio. There is little evidence to suggest that the noble idea or the song ever gained momentum.

There were concerns during the Columbus city song contest that a "devious song writer" might enter the competition using the University of Michigan fight song with different lyrics and stir political consequences.

85

THE BUILDING WITH A REPUTATION

Where is one of the most often-referenced buildings in downtown Columbus?

Few landmarks in Columbus have the reputation or history of the downtown Buggy Works building. Oftentimes, when giving directions, a downtowner might use the Buggy Works building on Nationwide Boulevard as a point of reference.

The notable historic building in the heart of the Arena District is currently a condominium development repurposed as part of a revitalization effort in the area. While the renovated warehouse receives a lot of attention, the meaning behind the nickname is largely overlooked.

In 1902, the building was the pulse of the Columbus Buggy Company. The original factory operating in the years prior was located at High Street and Hickory Alley. It eventually expanded to a new factory at 400 Dublin Avenue, now Nationwide Boulevard. It was one of the largest buggy manufacturers in the world, producing one every eight minutes. The company had one thousand employees cranking out buggies. Columbus Buggy Works became a force of influence in the nation's transportation system.

The competition created by automobiles in the early

Transportation moguls Edward Rickenbacker and Harvey Firestone honed their early business skills at the Columbus Buggy Company before moving on to other endeavors.

Redevelopment of the historic Buggy Works building has new life in the Arena District as condominiums.

twentieth century led to the company's demise. The company attempted to progress from horse-powered transportation to gas- and electric-powered vehicles, but they simply could not compete with the up-and-coming automobile manufacturers for customer interest. The Columbus Buggy Company filed for bankruptcy in 1913.

Over the decades, the Columbus "Buggy Works" building has evolved, serving many purposes, and it remains an iconic landmark that apartment and condo dwellers now call home.

THE COLUMBUS BUGGY COMPANY

WHAT One of the largest twentieth-century buggy manufacturers in the world, with a building that remains an iconic Columbus landmark

WHERE 448 Nationwide Blvd.

COST None

PRO TIP This prime property in downtown Columbus is within walking distance of Nationwide Arena, North Bank Park, the North Market, and the Short North.

86

MISSING ARTICLES ON CHRISTOPHER COLUMBUS

What key items are missing from the famed Italian explorer?

The Christopher Columbus statue located on the south side of the Ohio Statehouse in downtown Columbus is a fitting tribute to the Italian explorer after whom the city is named. Looking casually at the copper statue, it is unlikely that anyone would notice that the famed explorer is missing something. Actually, two things. Only someone who was familiar with the historical photographs might observe that Columbus is missing the calipers from his right hand and the dagger from his belt.

The statue was originally situated in the courtyard of the Pontifical College Josephinum at Main and 18th Streets. It was commissioned by Monsignor Joseph Jessing in 1892 to commemorate the 400th anniversary of Columbus's discovery of America.

When the Pontifical College relocated to Worthington in 1932, the statue was not included in the move. Instead, the college gifted it to the State of Ohio, where it found a permanent home on the statehouse plaza.

Somewhere during the move, Columbus lost some of his identifying accoutrements. It is not clear what happened

---

The Christopher Columbus Statue is made of hammered copper plates and was commissioned for $400 in 1892.

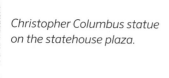

CHRISTOPHER COLUMBUS STATUE

WHAT The prominent statue commemorating the Italian explorer at the Ohio Statehouse is missing some of his original equipment.

WHERE The South Plaza on the Ohio Statehouse grounds

COST None

PRO TIP Take note of the etchings on the base of the statue, which commemorate notable Ohioans.

to those items, but very few people are aware that anything is missing.

In 1992 the statue obtained a new base commemorating the 500th anniversary of Columbus's voyage. During that time, the tarnished statue was freshened up to its original copper color, but Columbus's tools were never replaced.

Where are below-ground tunnels hiding more than just secret passageways?

As the pulse of city government beats in the corridors of City Hall, few public officials have any idea of what lingers below them. Many employees have only been to what they thought was the lowest level during tornado drills in the basement. But City Hall's roots go even deeper.

The sub-basement of City Hall is a fascinating glimpse into a time when America was under nuclear threat. This hidden section of the building consists of three corridors with low ceilings and reinforced concrete walls. It was Columbus's first air-raid shelter, outfitted for city employees in 1952. Most present-day employees do not even know it exists, and those who do are unlikely to know its original purpose.

A series of obstacles are scattered in the tight dim quarters, from old valves protruding from the sides of the narrow hallways to low-hanging water supply pipes, electrical conduit, and air ducts.

An area at the end of one corridor appears to be the main quick access entry point to the air-raid shelter. A small door, about half the height of a normal door, is on the wall in the

---

City Auditor Hugh Dorrian remembers seeing thousands of stored crackers and water drums in the sub-basement when he used the hallways to access adjacent buildings to City Hall in 1966.

A corridor in the air-raid shelter below ground where city employees would retreat during emergencies.

Inset: A small escape door from the stairwell of the City Hall basement for emergency access to the air-raid shelter below ground.

AIR-RAID SHELTER

WHAT The city's first air-raid shelter, which is still intact beneath City Hall

WHERE City Hall, downtown Columbus

COST None

PRO TIP The public is not allowed in the sub-basement, but you can visit City Hall.

basement-level stairwell. That leads to a steel ladder into the bunker below and a concrete platform that enabled employees to quickly drop to protective position in the corridors.

The widest corridor runs the length of City Hall and has higher ceilings. This section served as storage for thousands of crackers and fifty-five-gallon drums filled with water. Those stored items have since been removed.

In light of recent political developments, it would seem that the need for protection from nuclear attack might not be too far off the mark. Perhaps the city would be well-advised to update and refurbish this mysterious place to serve its original, suddenly practical purpose.

⁸⁸ SPRING A LEAK

What Columbus street has a soggy reputation?

When rain falls in Columbus, drivers do not even need to look at the sign for Spring Street in downtown to know their location. The street, which is one of the major thoroughfares through downtown Columbus, is named for the large amount of rushing water that once ran through that corridor.

The street bordered several springs and became the confluence of continually merging sources of water that eventually ended in the Scioto River. The rushing water that made its way through downtown is how Spring Street got its name.

The muddy ground in the area made for constant moving water along surrounding streets, like Broad Street, Fourth Street, Fifth Street, and High Street. The Spring and High intersection is where the culmination of water sources produced a rushing current in the early nineteenth century.

Horses could wade across the water, but it was too dangerous for pedestrians. Prior to 1830, Columbus residents used a primitive bridge made from two logs to cross north over the creek. The pedestrian bridge became a prime fishing spot for young boys.

While the only modern-day remnant of Spring Street's watery thoroughfare is its name on the sign, a hard Columbus rain and the subsequent flooding that still occurs is a quick reminder of how downtown used to be.

Spring Street runs through downtown Columbus.

While the names of many streets around downtown Columbus have changed over the years, Spring Street still has its original name.

SPRING STREET

WHAT One of many Columbus streets with a literal meaning behind its name

WHERE A main east-west corridor through downtown Columbus

COST None

PRO TIP Pass Spring Street during a rain storm to get a sense of how quickly water accumulated in the area in the 1800s.

BIBLIOGRAPHY

1. **Finders Keepers:** City of Columbus. Columbus Art Walks: Clintonville; Interview with artists Matthew Logsdon.

2. **Union Station Arches:** Arter, Bill. *Columbus Vignettes.* "Grand Entrance." Nita-Eckstein Printing, 1966. P. 59; Arter, Bill. *Columbus Vignettes II.* "Union Station." Nida-Eckstein Printing Inc., 1967. P. 13; Lentz, Ed. *As It Were: Stories of Old Columbus.* Red Mountain Press, 1998. P. 130; Thomas, Robert. *Columbus Unforgettables.* "How The Union Station Arch Was Saved," excerpt by Judge George C. Smith. Robert Thomas published, 1984. P. 231; The City of Columbus Recreation and Parks Department. "McFerson Commons Park." https://www.columbus.gov/recreationandparks/parks/McFerson-Commons-Park/

3. **Circus House Secrets:** Arter, Bill. *Columbus Vignettes.* "Peter and the Circus." Nita-Eckstein Printing, 1966. P. 42; Lentz, Ed. Historic Columbus, *A Bicentennial History.* Historical Publishing Network, 2011. P. 82; Patzer, Nancy. (2008, April 9). Circus Town! Sells Brothers' Show Called Columbus Home. *The Short North Gazette.* Weiker, Jim. (2017, February 5). Remodeled 'Circus House' Beside Goodale Park Energizes New Owner. *The Columbus Dispatch;* Information from site visit and interview with current owner Weston Wolfe.

4. **The Short North Name:** The Short North Arts District, http://shortnorth.org/. Information from interviews with Betsy Pandora, Executive Director, Short North Alliance and Lieutenant Karl Barth, Columbus Division of Police. Information from site visits. http://shortnorth.org/

5. **No Sweet Tooth on Sunday:** Ohio State Supreme Court Law Library. General Ordinances of the City of Columbus. January 1, 1882. Gazette Printing and Publishing House, 1882. P. 153.

6. ***Columbus Dispatch* News Ticker:** "Timeline: History of *The Columbus Dispatch.*" http://www.dispatch.com/content/stories/local/2016/07/01/dispatch-timeline.html. 30 June 2016; "A front-page history of *The Columbus Dispatch.*" Ohio Newspaper Association. 2015.

7. **World's First Junior High School:** Arter, Bill. *Columbus Vignettes IV.* "World's First." Nida-Eckstein Printing Inc., 1971. P. 28; City of Columbus. Columbus Art Walks: Clintonville; Columbus Landmarks Foundation. "Indianola Middle School." http://columbuslandmarks.org/preservation/advocacy/indianola-middle-school/; Thomas, Robert. *More Columbus Unforgettables.* Robert Thomas published, 1986. P. 317.

8. **Where the Insane Are Forgotten:** Paulson, George W, MD, and Sherman, Marion E., MD. *Hilltop: A Hospital and a Sanctuary for Healing, its Past and its Future.* Lesher Printers, 2008. Information from site visits.

9. **Tigers Aren't Just at the Zoo:** *Columbus Dispatch.* "Exotic-animal facility seeks case." 5 November 2015. http://www.dispatch.com/content/stories/local/2015/11/05/more-money-needed-so-state-can-care-for-transport-exotic-animals.html; *Columbus Dispatch.* "Sheriff: 56 exotic animals escaped from farm near Zanesville; 49 killed by authorities." http://www.dispatch.com/article/20111018/NEWS/310189714. 18 October 2011; Ohio Department of Agriculture. "Dangerous Wild Animal Temporary Holding Facility Fact Sheet.

10. **World's First Suburban Strip Mall:** Allcolumbusdata.com. "Columbus Retail History Part #2: Shopping Centers." 22 January 2013. http://allcolumbusdata.com/?p=245; Mueller-Kuhnert, Laura. *Columbus, Ohio: A Trivia Look.* "World's First Regional Strip Mall." Old #8 Press, Inc. 1984. P. 25; Ohio History Connection. "Shopping Centers." *Ohio History Central.* http://www.ohiohistorycentral.org/w/Shopping_Centers; Ohio History Connection. "Town and Country Shopping Center." *Ohio History Central.* http://www.ohiohistorycentral.org/w/Town_and_Country_Shopping_Center

11. **"Carmen Ohio" Lyrics:** Songs of The Ohio State University website. "Carmen Ohio." http://www.sgsosu.net/osu/songs/carmen_ohio.html; Thomas, Robert. *More Columbus Unforgettables.* Robert Thomas published, 1986. P. 82.

12. **Home of the Slider:** Hogan, David Gerard. Selling 'em by the Sack. NYU Press, 1999; Ingram, E.W. All T*his from a 5-cent Hamburger.* Princeton University Press, 1964; Interviews with White Castle marketing executives.

13. **Nineteenth-Century Amusements:** Barrett, Richard. *Columbus and Central Ohio Historian, No.1.* "Olentangy Park." Published by Richard Barrett, 1984. P. 5; City of Columbus. Columbus Art Walks: Clintonville. https://www.columbus.gov/publichealth/programs/Healthy-Places/Art-Walks/Clintonville-Art-Walk/; Lentz, Ed. Historic Columbus: *A Bicentennial History.* Historical Publishing network, 2011. P. 83; Sway. "Olentangy Park" report. https://sway.com/06T2EbvnO7DWPUU4

14. **The Best Open-Air View of Columbus:** Ohio.gov. Department of Administrative Services. "Rhodes Tower." http://das.ohio.gov/Divisions/GeneralServices/PropertiesandFacilities/Rhodes.aspx; Ohio History Connection. "James A. Rhodes." *Ohio History Central.* http://www.ohiohistorycentral.org/w/James_A._Rhodes; Interviews with Tom Hoyt, Chief Communications officer, Ohio Department of Administrative Services; Personal site visit.

15. **A Stroll Down Memory Lane:** City of Columbus. Columbus Art Walks: Clintonville. https://www.columbus.gov/publichealth/programs/Healthy-Places/Art-Walks/Clintonville-Art-Walk/; Interview with Clintonville Historical Society.

16. **The Original Mr. Peanut:** *The Columbus Dispatch.* "Peanut Shoppe will move a few blocks, expecting more foot traffic." http://www.dispatch.com/article/20140308/news/303089907. 8 March 2014; Interview with Pat Stone, owner of the Peanut Shoppe.

17. **The Pagoda Mystery:** Arter, Bill. *Columbus Vignettes.* "Oriental Mystery." Nida-Eckstein Printing, 1966. P. 68; Essley, Joffre. *Columbus Underground.*com. "The Most Unusual Building in Columbus." 26 November 2013. http://www.columbusunderground.com/the-most-unusual-building-in-columbus-je1; Interview with John Capretta, VP Columbus Firefighters Local 67 and site visit; Waymarking.com. "Toledo and Ohio Central Railroad Station – Columbus, Ohio." 16 January 2011. http://www.waymarking.com/waymarks/WMAHDA_Toledo_and_Ohio_Central_Railroad_Station_Columbus_OH

18. **Secret Maze below Campus:** *Columbus Monthly.* "Secret Columbus: Wonders That Are Hidden in Plain Sight." 13 October 2014; Hershey, Linda. *The Ohio State Lantern.* "Tunnels Feed OSU." 23 October 1969; Infiltration.com. The Ohio State University Steam Tunnels. http://www.infiltration.org/underosu/tunnels.html; Outland, J. Danbridge. *The Ohio State Lantern.* "Tunnels service OSU." 6 August 1973; Pena, Chris. Ocolly.com. Mythbusters: Are there tunnels under OSU's campus? http://www.ocolly.com/news/article_220954b6-2d66-11e4-b2ca-001a4bcf6878.html; Interview with OSU Marketing Department.

19. **Polynesian Memories and Memorabilia:** Kahiki.com. "The Kahiki Story: The Legend Lives On." http://www.kahiki.com/story/; Lang, Emily. Ohio History Connection Blog. "The Kahiki Supper Club." January 2014; https://www.ohiohistory.org/learn/collections/history/history-blog/2014/january-2014/the-kahiki-supper-club; Motz, Doug. *Columbus Underground.* "History Lesson: The history of Columbus's most famed 'lost' restaurant – The Kahiki." http://www.columbusunderground.com/history-lesson-the-history-of-columbus-most-famed-lost-restaurant-the-kahiki. 11 September 2012; Interview with Sarah Bogan, Kahiki spokesperson.

20. **When Outdoor Concerts Rocked Columbus:** Ball, Brian. *Columbus Business First.* Ikea eyes Polaris for next Ohio store. 26 January 2015; *Columbus Monthly.* "Secret Columbus: Wonders That Are Hidden in Plain Sight." 13 October 2014.

21. **Right Soldier, Wrong Name:** Congressional Medal of Honor Society. Roy, Stanislaus. http://www.cmohs.org/recipient-detail/1861/roy-stanislaus.php; Homeofheroes.com. Stanislaus Roy. Personal site visit to grave.

22. **The Narrowing Road:** The Baist atlases for 1899, 1910, and 1920; Betti, Tom, Lentz, Ed and Uhas Sauer, Doreen. *Columbus Neighborhoods: A Guide to the Landmarks of Franklinton, German Village, King-Lincoln, Olde Town East, Short North & the University District.* The History Press, 2013. P. 67; Miller, Maude Murray. Interview with Betsy Pandora, Executive Director of the Short North Alliance; Interview with Nick Montell, owner, the Greystone Building.

23. **Supreme Justice:** Columbus Art Walks: River South; Supremecourtofohio.com. "The Contemporary Art of the Thomas J. Moyer Ohio Judicial Center." https://www.supremecourt.ohio.gov/VisitorInfo/art/; The Supreme Court of Ohio. *The Thomas J. Moyer Ohio Judicial Center.* P. 35.

24. **Home of the Buckeyes:** Ohio History Connection. "Columbus Bicentennial: Gloria Hoover Markets the Edible Buckeye." 1 February 2012. http://columbusbicentennial.blogspot.com/2012/02/gloria-hoover-markets-edible-buckeye.html

25. *Brushstrokes in Flight:* Tebben Gerald. 14 March 2012. Columbus Mileposts | March 14, 1984: Maligned airport artwork got no respect – at first. *The Columbus Dispatch;* Thomas, Robert. *More Columbus Unforgettables.* Robert Thomas published, 1986. P. 305; Flycolumbus.com. Art Displays. http://flycolumbus.com/at-port-columbus/art-displays/.

26. **Downtown Television:** Anietra Hamper's first-hand knowledge from being involved in the development and operation of *NBC4 on the Square.*

27. **Out of Place:** Arter, Bill. *Columbus Vignettes* II. "Flatiron Building" Nida-Eckstein Printing Inc., 1967. P. 15; The Ohio State University Explore Columbus Blog. "The Flatiron." 28 November 2016. https://u.osu.edu/explorecolumbus/author/slonsky-2/; Wikipedia. Flatiorn Building. www.en.wikipedia.org/wiki/Flatiron_Building.

28. **The Careful Flow of Waste:** Tebben, Gerald. *The Columbus Dispatch.* "Columbus Mileposts | April 18, 1853: Cholera, fires spur municipal water system." 18 April 2012; The City of Columbus. Wastewater Treatment in Columbus. https://www.columbus.gov/utilities/about/Wastewater-Treatment-in-Columbus/

29. **Flytown:** Bishop, Anna. *The Black Experience in Columbus Ohio.* Contributor Daft, Betty. "There's little left of old Flytown." P. 105. Contributor Edwards, Randall. "Flytowners remember their neighborhood in its heyday." P. 107; Columbus Department of Slum Clearance and Rehabilitation. "A Report of a Study of Improvements for Sewers, Water Lines, Streets, and Street Lighting for the Goodale Slum Clearance Project." 1957; Howard, Arnett. *Columbus Bicentennial* blog. "Columbus Bicentennial: Flytown: Northwest Columbus. 03 January 2012. http://columbusbicentennial.blogspot.com/2012/01/flytown-northwest-columbus.html; Smith, Toni, MD and Lentz, Ed. Columbus Landmarks Foundation report of African-American Settlements and Communities in Columbus, Ohio. "Flytown." Columbus Landmarks Foundation Press, 2014. P. 44.

30. **Columbus's Flag Flap:** Bradshaw, James. *The Columbus Dispatch.* "City Is Illogical Vexillologically." 20 August 1974. P. 1-B; City of Columbus. 1912 Coat of Arms Resolution. 1912; City of Columbus. Letter to Mayor Tom Moody from Chief of Police. 14 February 1975; *The Columbus Dispatch.* "Columbus's Flag Official – at Last." 27 February 1975; *The Columbus Dispatch.* "Columbus Now Has Official Flag." 21 December 1928. P. 2-B; *The Journal of Great Waters Association of Vexillology.* December 1998. Vol. III, No. 2: Issue 6; Meekins, John. Columbus Citizen Journal. "Moody Unfurls City Banner." 23 March 1976. P. 1; Ruth, Robert. *The Columbus Dispatch Sunday Magazine.* "Only Two Known Copies Exist, Our City Flag." 10 June 1973. P. 12.

31. **Nostalgic Downtown Sandwich:** Thomas, Robert. *More Columbus Unforgettables.* "A Glorious and Famous Sandwich." Robert Thomas published, 1986. P. 151.

32. **Historically Squirrelly Behavior:** Tebben Gerald. 19 April 2012. Columbus Mileposts | April 19, 1822: Settlers showed ravenous squirrels no mercy. *The Columbus Dispatch;* Lentz, Ed. *This Week Community News.* "Squirrels ran amok in early 1800s." 2 February 2015; Ohio Department of Natural wildlife. Gray Squirrel. http://wildlife.ohiodnr.gov/species-and-habitats/species-guide-index/mammals/eastern-gray-squirrel; Ohio History Connection. "Grand Squirrel Hunt: August 31, 1822." *Ohio History Central.* 3 January 2012.

33. **Famous Unknown Boy Scout:** The Ohio Statehouse. Boy Scouts 75th and Unknown Boy Scout. http://www.ohiostatehouse.org/galleries/media/boy-scouts-75th-and-unknown-boy-scout.

34. **Housing More Than Military Supplies:** Defense Supply Center Columbus. https://dsccmwr.com/; Local knowledge of location.

35. **Ringside Treasure:** Benton, G.A. "Classic Columbus Haunts: Ringside Café." http://www.columbusalive.com/article/20101006/lifestyle/310069227. 6 October 2010; Ringside Café. http://www.ringsidecolumbus.com.

36. **His Lips Are Sealed:** *Columbus Bicentennial* blog. "The Death of Leatherlips, Wyandot Indian Chief." 03 January 2012. http://columbusbicentennial.blogspot.com/2012/01/death-of-leatherlips-wyandote-indian.html; Gurvis, Sandra. *Ohio Curiosities: Quirky Characters, Roadside Oddities & Other Offbeat Stuff.* Globe Pequot Press, 2011. P. 224-225; Thomas, Robert. Columbus Unforgettables. Robert Thomas published, 1984. P. 220.

37. **A Big Impression:** Friends of the Topiary Park. www.topiarypark.org; Information from site visits.

38. **No Dome:** The Ohio Statehouse. www.ohiostatehouse.org; Interview with Ohio Statehouse Media Relations.

39. **A Display of Champions:** Thomas, Robert. *More Columbus Unforgettables.* Robert Thomas published, 1986. P.296.

40. **National Road Nostalgia:** Interview with Ohio National Road Association; Ohio National Road Association. http://www.ohionationalroad.org/; Thomas, Robert. Columbus Unforgettables. "A Rare National Road Original Stone Milepost." Robert Thomas published, 1984. P. 223; Wallace, James. *Columbus Monthly.* "The National Road." December 1980; P. 149.

41. **Swine-Inspired Landfills:** Meckstroth, Kenneth. *Columbus Grows Up*, published in Ohio State Journal. "Rubbish and Garbage Disposal." Columbus, 1951. P. 50-53; Interview Hanna Greer-Brown, Communications Manager, SWACO.

42. **Scandal Tips the Scales of Justice:** *Columbus Dispatch.* "Bostwick Family." 10 June 1934 in Show Section; Thomas, Robert. *More Columbus Unforgettables*. Robert Thomas published, 1986. P. 142-143; *TIME Magazine.* "Indian-Giving Judge." 5 October 1931; Court documents from Franklin County Probate Court on Bostwick's removal.

43. **Railroad Car Sanctuary:** The Deport Rail Museum website and interview. http://the-depot.org/wordpress/

44. **Smelly Success:** OSU Biological Sciences Greenhouse. https://bioscigreenhouse.osu.edu/; Interview with biologist Joan Leonard.

45. **Cutting-Edge Community:** Forest Park Civic Association. https://www.fpcivic.org/; Personal site visits.

46. **A District Fit for a King:** Betti, Tom, Lentz, Ed and Uhas Sauer, Doreen. *Columbus Neighborhoods: A Guide to the Landmarks of Franklinton, German Village, King-Lincoln, Olde Town East, Short North & the University District*. The History Press, 2013. P. 120; Nice, Walter. 21 April 2010. Brewing Royalty. *Columbus Dispatch*; Personal site visits.

47. **Cover That Up:** Columbus City Codes 1959. Adopted by Ordinance 1-59. The City Bulletin. P. 34A.

48. **Take Me Out to the Ball Game:** Santry, Joe and the Columbus Clippers. "14 things you didn't know about baseball in Columbus." Columbus Alive. http://www.columbusalive.com/content/stories/2015/04/09/14-things-you-didnt-know-about-baseball-in-columbus.html. 8 April 2015; ClippersBaseball.com. History of baseball in Columbus. http://www.milb.com/content/page.jsp?ymd=20090317&content_id=40997452&sid=t445&vkey=team2

49. **More Than Miracles Inside the Grotto:** City of Columbus. Columbus Art Walks: Clintonville; Pannell, Mary. "Grotto." *Catholic Times*, shared in the Immaculate Conception newsletter.

50. **Pieces of the Old Ohio Pen:** Fontaine, Tom. TribLive publication from Nationwide. "Columbus provides blueprint for how to develop Mellon Arena site." *TribLive.* 5 October 2014; *The Arena District: A Neighborhood 170 Years in the Making*. Published by Nationwide Realty Investors, 2006.

51. **Segregated Socializing:** Interview with Christy Evans, Gahanna Historical Society and personal site visit.

52. **Columbus's First Zoo:** *Columbus Monthly.* "Secret Columbus: Wonders That Are Hidden in Plain Sight." 13 October 2014; Hayes, Christine. Columbus Bicentennial blog. "Columbus Bicentennial: Early Columbus Zoo." 11 June 2012. http://columbusbicentennial.blogspot.com/2012/06/early-columbus-zoo.html; Roshon, Sam. Clintonvillehistory.com. "From Evolution to Extinction an Early Zoo in Columbus." 1987. http://clintonvillehistory.com/wp-content/uploads/zoo-winter-87.pdf.

53. **Dancing Rabbits of Ballantrae Park:** Ballantrae-Dublin. http://www.ballantrae-dublin.com/dancinghares.aspx.

54. **Glass Myth:** Arter, Bill. *Columbus Vignettes.* "Tropics Under Glass." Nita-Eckstein Printing, 1966. P. 78; Interview with Franklin Park Conservatory.

55. **Columbus's Royal Wedding:** Betti, Tom, Lentz, Ed and Uhas Sauer, Doreen. *On This Day in Columbus, Ohio History*. The History Press, 2013. P. 152; Motz, Doug. ColumbusUnderground.com. "History Lesson: A Royal Wedding in Columbus." 16 May 2012. http://www.columbusunderground.com/history-lesson-a-royal-wedding-in-columbus; Viviano, JoAnne. 10 September 2012. Time Travel in Schiller Park. *Columbus Dispatch*; Interview with Barry Weber, former Columbus Forrester; Personal site visit.

56. **Coming Up Roses:** Lentz, Ed. *As It Were: Stories of Old Columbus.* Red Mountain Press, 1998. P. 130; Mueller-Kuhnert, Laura. *Columbus, Ohio: A Trivia Look.* Old #8 Press, Inc. 1984. P. 176; Personal site visits.

57. **Magic beyond the Grave:** Meyers, David and Walker, Elise Meyers. *Wicked Columbus, Ohio.* History Press, 2015. P. 69-75; Ross, John. "Creating Columbus 1896- 1918." *Columbus Alive.* http://www.columbusalive.com/content/stories/2012/02/02/creating-columbus-1896-1918.html; 2 February 2012; Steinmeyer, Jim. *The Last Greatest Magician in the World.* The Penguin Group, 2011; Personal site visit.

58. **Hidden Civil War Cemetery:** Lentz, Ed. Historic Columbus: *A Bicentennial History.* Historical Publishing Network, 2011. P. 57; National Park Service. "Camp Chase Confederate Cemetery Columbus, Ohio." https://www.nps.gov/nr/travel/national_cemeteries/Ohio/Camp_Chase_Confederate_Cemetery.html

59. **Undying Devotion:** Decker, Theodore. *The Columbus Dispatch.* "Theodore Decker Commentary: Old pet cemetery shows signs of love, wear." 17 November 2016. http://www.dispatch.com/content/stories/local/2016/11/17/memories-of-faithful-friend-live-on-at-pet-cemetery.html; Personal site visit; *RoadsideAmerica.com.* "Columbus, Ohio: Brown Pet Cemetery: Sgt. Fleabite Smith, et al." 3 March 2015. http://www.roadsideamerica.com/tip/14239.

60. **Concrete Corn:** Dublin Arts Council. "Field of Corn with Osage Oranges." https://dublinarts.org/featured-items/fieldofcorn/?portfolioCats=94.

61. **Remnants of Aviation History:** Columbus Landmarks Foundation. "Endangered No.1 – Port Columbus Airport Control Tower." http://columbuslandmarks.org/preservation/columbus-airport-control-tower/; *Columbus Monthly.* "Secret Columbus: Wonders That Are Hidden in Plain Sight." 13 October 2014; Thebault, Reis. "Work Begins on Old Port Columbus Terminal." *Columbus Dispatch.* 21 July 2015. http://www.dispatch.com/content/stories/local/2015/07/21/Work-begins-on-old-Port-Columbus-terminal.html; Interview with Angie Tabor, John Glenn International Airport

62. **Lone Skyscraper:** Kamau, Kojo. Columbus Remembered. Lulu Press, 2006; Mueller-Kuhnert, Laura. *Columbus, Ohio, A Trivia Look.* Old #8 Press, Inc., 1984. P. 10; Lentz, Ed. *As It Were: Stories of Old Columbus.* Red Mountain Press, 1998. P. 168.

63. **Columbus–Bike Friendly Before It Was Cool:** CoGo Bike Share. https://www.cogobikeshare.com/; Langdon, Alvin. *First Events in Columbus.* Columbus Research Bureau, 1946. P. 35; The City of Columbus. "Bicycling." https://www.columbus.gov/publicservice/Bicycle-Program/.

64. **Scottish Sounds in the Neighborhood:** Capitalcitypipesanddrums.com. http://www.capitalcitypipesanddrums.com/index.html; Interview with Jay of Capital City Pipes and Drums.

65. **Feed Sack Flare:** Rose, Marla. "Revamped North Market to include 35-story tower as centerpiece." *The Columbus Dispatch.* 12 April 2017. http://www.dispatch.com/news/20170412/revamped-north-market-to-include-35-story-tower-as-centerpiece; Interview with Rick Harrison Wolfe, Executive Director of North Market; Personal site visits.

66. **Lustron Homes:** Ohio History Connection. "Lustron Homes." *Ohio History Central*. http://www.ohiohistorycentral.org/w/Lustron_Homes; Thornton, Rosemary. "Lustron Homes." Old House Web. http://www.oldhouseweb.com/architecture-and-design/lustron-homes-part-1.shtml

67. **Highest Point:** Arter, Bill. *Columbus Vignettes II*. "Highest Elevation in Columbus." Nida-Eckstein Printing Inc., 1967. P. 21; Historical Marker Project. http://www.historicalmarkerproject.com/markers/HMB2Q_st-paul-african-methodist-episcopal-church_Columbus-OH.html; Interviews with James Goodenow, Director, Franklin County Public Facilities Management and BenMcCown, Chief Cartographer, Franklin County Engineer's Office.

68. **Road to Nowhere:** Interview with Andy Beard, Cols Engineering Section; Interview with Nancy Burton, ODOT; Personal site visit.

69. **What's in a Name?:** Friends of Goodale Park. http://goodalepark.org/; Lentz, Ed. *As It Were: Stories of Old Columbus*. Red Mountain Press, 1998. P. 12-15.

70. **Cautious Crossing:** City of Columbus. Columbus Art Walks: Clintonville; This Week Community News, Dublin. "Council picks $460K pedestrian underpass design." 16 December 2014. http://www.thisweeknews.com/content/stories/dublin/news/2014/12/16/riverside-drive-realignment-council-picks-460k-pedestrian-underpass-design.html; Personal site visit.

71. **Creative Space:** Personal site visit and interview with Todd Camp of the Cultural Arts Center of Columbus.

72. **Patriotic Rock:** Fitzpatrick, Stephen *A. History of Columbus Celebration, Franklinton Centennial*. The New Franklin Printing Company, 1897; Personal site visit.

73. **OSU's Non-Fraternity Fraternity:** Corbett, John. *More Columbus Unforgettables*. "SI-U Keeps Old Friendships Alive." Robert Thomas published, 1986. P. 78.

74. **Lost Capitol Cornerstone:** Davis, Marilyn Clifton. *Ohio's Statehouse Is Intriguing*. Published by Marilyn Clifton Davis, 1999. P. 75; Lentz, Ed. *As It Were: Stories of Old Columbus*. Red Mountain Press, 1998. P. 20-23.

75. **A Brick among Bricks:** Personal site visits and interview with Brioso Roastery & Coffee Bar Owner, Jeff Davis.

76. **Red-light District Vanishes:** Betti, Tom, Lentz, Ed and Uhas Sauer, Doreen. *On This Day in Columbus, Ohio History*. The History Press, 2013. P. 18; Giffin, William. *African Americans and the Color Line in Ohio*, 1915-1930. Ohio State University Press, 2005. P. 23; Lentz, Ed. *This Week Community News*. "Vice found home in city's Badlands." 30 September 2014.

77. **Campus Cabin:** Arter, Bill. *Columbus Vignettes*. "David Beers' Cabin." Nita-Eckstein Printing, 1966. P. 81; Weiker, Jim. *The Columbus Dispatch*. "Oldest known home in Columbus: 208 years logged." 12 February 2012.

78. **Wartime Performances:** Mueller-Kuhnert, Laura. Columbus, Ohio: A Trivia Look. Old #8 Press, Inc. 1984. P. 24; Personal site visits and interview with Rolanda Copley, CAPA.

79. **Invention Hub:** Battelle.org. https://www.battelle.org/; Interview with Battelle Media Relations

80. **Mysterious Cloaked Statue:** Interview with German Village Society.

81. **Shimmy-Shake:** Habeeba's Dance of the Arts. http://habeebas.com/; Interview with Melissa Caldwell of Habeeba's Dance of the Arts Studio; Personal site visit and knowledge of local studios.

82. **Time-Out:** Highbanks Metro Park. http://www.metroparks.net/parks-and-trails/highbanks/; Personal site visits.

83. **Cow Town:** American Dairy Association interview with Karen Bakies; *History of Columbus Calendar* 1993 (Jan. 30, 1945); Ohio History Connection. "Ross Laboratories." *Ohio History Central*. http://www.ohiohistorycentral.org/w/Ross_Laboratories; *The Columbus Dispatch*. "Elsie the Cow, mascot of Borden dairy products." 9 March 2015. http://www.dispatch.com/content/stories/life_and_entertainment/2015/03/17/mascot-madness/elsie.html

84. **Columbus City Anthem:** *Columbus Citizen Journal*. "City Gets Official Song." 07 May 1966; Columbus Citizen Journal. "Two Rivers' Chosen As Columbus's Anthem." 07 May 1966; *Columbus Citizen Journal*. "City Songs Submitted." 06 March 1966; Reed, Jo. *Columbus Citizen Journal*. "City Song Contest Judging Friday." 06 May 1966; Roberts, George. *Columbus Citizen Journal*. "$500 Prize Offered for City Song." 29 December 1965. P. 1.

85. **The Building with a Reputation:** Arter, Bill. *Columbus Vignettes III & Columbus Closeups*. "The Buggy Works." Nida-Eckstein Printing Inc., 1969. P. 65; Ohio History Connection. "Columbus Buggy Company." *Ohio History Central*. http://www.ohiohistorycentral.org/w/Columbus_Buggy_Company; Thebuggyworkslofts.com. http://www.thebuggyworkslofts.com/; TouringOhio.com. "Columbus Buggy Company." http://touringohio.com/central/franklin/columbus/columbus-buggy.html.

86. **Missing Articles on Christopher Columbus:** Kuhnert, Laura. Columbus, Ohio: A Trivia Look. "World's First Regional Strip Mall." Old #8 Press, Inc. 1984. P. 22; The Ohio Statehouse. "Statues and Monuments – Christopher Columbus Discovery Monument." http://www.ohiostatehouse.org/about/capitol-square/statues-and-monuments/christopher-columbus-discovery-monument; Touring Ohio. "Discovery Plaza." http://touringohio.com/central/franklin/columbus/columbus-statue.html; Personal site visits.

87. **Under Cover:** Interview with Hugh Dorrian, Columbus City Auditor; Personal site visit to sub-basement shelter at City Hall.

88. **Spring a Leak:** Hooper, Osman Castle. *History of the city of Columbus, Ohio, from the founding of Franklinton in 1797, through the World War period to the year 1920*. Memorial Publishing Company, 1920. P. 27-32; Lentz, Ed. *This Week Community News*. "The naming of Columbus streets." 6 February 2013. http://www.thisweeknews.com/article/20130206/NEWS/302069549; Moore, Kathleen. Document compilation "A Capital City is Located and Becomes a City." P. 30-31.

INDEX